PEBBLES

PEBBLES

JULIE ANN SMITH

authorHOUSE®

AuthorHouse™ UK Ltd.
1663 Liberty Drive
Bloomington, IN 47403 USA
www.authorhouse.co.uk
Phone: 0800.197.4150

Published by AuthorHouse   02/20/2014

ISBN: 978-1-4918-9419-4 (sc)
ISBN: 978-1-4918-9420-0 (e)

CONTENTS

EPIGRAPH

Do not run outside for better seeing,
nor peer from a window.
Rather abide at the centre of your being . . . .
Excerpt from Lao Tzu

DEDICATION

For my supportive and loving husband Mike—my best friend—who in giving himself generously, allows me to feel secure and truly cared for. Not to mention, his photographic skills which produced the inspiring artwork for this book cover! For our three dear sons, Derren, Gary and Craig for enriching my life. For our lovely daughter-in-law Tori and 'daughter' Rainie, and grand-daughters, Alexia, Coralie and Emilia. For Cheryl, my sister-friend, my brother Graeme and Mary and all my other wonderful friends and family. And lastly for my dear parents, Joan and Ron, daily in my memory, for happy childhood memories.

Thank you all for being the most special parts of my life and through loving you, and sharing your lives, helping me discover who I am still becoming.

PREFACE

Throughout my life I have been very fortunate to enjoy extensive world-wide travel and adventures mostly with my husband, sometimes with my mum, and frequently with our three sons as they were growing up.

Discovering new places, fascinating architecture, amazing history and customs and seeing people participate in whichever culture they are influenced by, is one of my passions. I thirst for the knowledge and experience of varying landscapes, breath-taking sights and varied cultures that exist in our amazing world. The brief connections stay with me, subtly shaping my thinking and sense of who I am.

Having shared the fun and the challenges of having three sons, my husband and I now enjoy spending time with our increasing family of partners, grandchildren and friends, which is further fodder for my observations and insights, as I continue to learn of my tolerances and indulgences

Living in Cornwall where the rugged cliffs and beautiful beaches give the time and space to absorb more of the natural and spiritual connection I seek, combined with my lifelong active interest and participation in yoga, crystals, healing, metaphysics, spiritual connection and human psychology have all influenced the culmination of this, my first publication.

Recent stormy conditions hurled beautiful coloured pebbles on to a nearby pristine sandy beach transforming it with natural debris that focused the eyes to look intently at individual stones. Just as randomly, as pebbles tossed on to the shore, so life reveals itself to us, not as consecutive steps, but through unrelated episodes that have related meaning. That cohesive element gave me the courage to draw into focus a selection of articles which may appear to be unrelated but have the connection of life running through their messages. '**Pebbles**' was born.

Experiences throughout my life have prompted me to think and write about them in order to have a better understanding of their messages; and so by considering the options, make wiser choices. I've spoken from the heart about some of the dilemmas of daily living and how to address them. How in the confusion of life, we can choose to clear a path, enabling us to cope and become a better version of ourselves.

My basis for writing **Pebbles** is empathy, insight and desire to help anyone use more of their potential to really live well, with awareness, taking action that helps them enjoy their evolution.

Dip in as the mood takes you.

I wish you 'joie de vie'.

INTRODUCTION

Everything has a hidden meaning if you care to look.

You are a process of diversity and discovery and deserve to value your worth.

Are we Evolving or Recycling? Do we want to find new ways, or the same old, same old? What is working for us and what would we change? Could we get better results if we knew how?

Life is an unending series of choices. The choices we make uncover who we are, piece by piece.

Think about it. Because Thinking precedes Action. And we all take action in life, unless we are stuck.

Section One—**Becoming You**, is an exploration of some of the things which keep us stuck, avoiding change, and ever circling without progression. Procrastination, Courage, Communication, Change are just a few of the topics covered because their understanding is key to moving forward. **Becoming you**—because we are always evolving, never truly complete. You are a process of diversity and discovery and deserve to value your worth.

Section Two—**Is It Possible**? Abandon the need to work at getting it right, and just come along for the ride, as you suspend the idea of how things seem, in exchange for possibilities. Everything has a hidden meaning if you care to look. Hopefully some articles may make you smile, or better still, provoke a desire in you to look more closely at the connections you make.

Section Three—**Thinking Deeply**

This small offering is just a taste of the depth of thought required for us to see beyond the mundane. TIME and LIFE have been fathomed for millennia—see if you agree or disagree with my perception. I like debate! GRADUALLY FORGETTING was inspired by the thought that we are linked to our past by our memories—a storehouse of sights, sounds, faces and adventures, but how would you feel if the details began to slip away? If what you had taken for granted as your past was difficult to recall. You would still be you, in many aspects, but your world would look quite different. You would want the people around you to understand, even though the right words may not present themselves.

Authors note:

The start of anything is rarely its beginning, so delve into this book as your curiosity demands. Hopefully, somewhere along the way you will find comfort, connection, direction or even criticism to debate or ponder. If your curiosity has been satisfied in a way that lingers and leads you to finding your own Pebbles, so much the better!

SECTION 1

BECOMING YOU

PROCRASTINATION

It is difficult to read this article isn't it? It's something about that word that makes you feel guilty. As if each of us knows it's a part of life we'd prefer not to bother with, or at least not just now!! Why in fact did anyone come up with a definition for a lack of an action which we'd prefer not to bother with at the moment. Why couldn't all the things we would rather not tackle now just slide into the unseen. Perhaps they would melt away and we would never have to deal with them. Just let life take over. It does anyway, and tomorrow there will be a whole new series of things 'to do', which can be put off as well. How about an invisible 'in-tray' building in the ether where they can be ignored?. Anyway, if this lot is cleared, chances are that tomorrow there will be more to fill their place, so where's the win situation in that?

No, best leave that long word to its own devices and get on . . . and chill out!

Trouble is I have got a few things to do, and although they won't take long it means me spending my precious 'free' time doing what I consider chores instead of pleasures . . . Oh alright I'll make the phone call . . . . now where did I put the number . . . its engaged . . .

good, I'll ring another time—at least I tried! Back to the couch . . .

Familiar scenario? Well it is for most of us!

We have busy lives which are already pressurised so it's natural to want to get away from the pressures of what we need to do, and tackle what we want to do instead . . . Although that choice seems feasible the inner voice which is preparing us for the next of life's events is a worrier that has its finger on the *Get It Done Now* button, and does not give up until it has its way.

So the simple advice coming up . . . (yes, all those sighs which signal the raising of the drawbridge of resistance, can be heard) will enable you to deal with getting the one or two things you know you have to do, DONE! Won't that be a nice relief?

The fact that you know you have to do them imminently is because they have been hanging over you, for some time now, and there is an imperative to act. You can't actually delay any longer (more's the pity).

You will see, that *procrastination* is actually the breathing space we give ourselves (particularly when our lives are stressful and rushed) to reconsider options, to prioritise; and to decide on a time for action. However the option we are most likely to consider is the option to let the action slip away! Hmmm!

Some things do actually fall off the end of a list—because we've not tackled it, it's not so imperative now—oh hang on—you don't actually have a list? Ah! So you've got a good memory, right? No! You'd prefer to forget all the things you have to do? Wouldn't we all, but with life's pleasures, come life's *responsibilities*. Probably another word it would have been preferable not to have been invented.

So where are we? Life is going along and, for instance, a bill arrives. You can tell it's a bill 'cos its official looking, and your birthday is not for another few months, so you'll look at it tonight (when you've got more time). Tonight comes: boy, that was a busy day! All I want to do now is relax and chill out! Morning again, the postman has been and there's a bit of junk mail and another official looking letter. Bet it's another bill! No time now, look tonight. Arrangements for tonight mean you have to be looking your best by 7pm and it's already 6pm . . . no time for the mail, I'll do it tomorrow.

Tomorrow finally comes. Although you are unaware of the inner deliberations, your mind has been trying to deceive your will from doing the right thing by setting up a disrupting event which will protect you from the consequence of not getting the job done. Complicated, yes! Here it is. Right I'll just get a coffee, make sure the fire's on, the football begins in 10 minutes, I'll just open the letters. Oh hang on, what's that, that can't be right. I never used the phone for that many calls. And what's this, a bill for dry cleaning? That was months ago; I thought I'd paid that one! Blow! Oh that will have to wait, the football's just starting, and I deserve to chill out and enjoy this match. So, bills to coffee table, probably not looked at again that day.

Anyway, eventually it is necessary to pick up one of the bills. In frustration, because your mind has been allowed time to accumulate the possible scenario you will now have to go through, a lump of resentment lodges as you realise you may well have made that many calls, or not paid the dry cleaning bill. So you hunt rooms, drawers, etc trying to find verification for the bills or not, and then decide to call the company. Too late, the hours of opening are passed, and the frustration has to melt away until another time. So your good intention of dealing with this, has been sabotaged (not your fault though, you did try).

You can see a pattern emerging. And yes, sometimes life is exactly like this whether we try to arrange it differently or not. However, it is worthwhile trying a different strategy in order to change the frustration caused by not taking action, to pride in getting the job done in a timely manner. To change from the overwhelming feeling that things are building up, to coping with a smaller manageable list. From being unreliable to being reliable, with a justified sense of achievement

So what's on your mind right now? Make a list of the things you know you should do. Really hate to burden you further, but this may include events you need to prepare for, like a special event coming up (birthday, anniversary) as well as jobs you need to get done, bills to be paid, emails to be sent, etc.

Look at the list and take two of the most important and imminent. Knowing your record, give yourself a chance to succeed by dating them at least four days in advance of when they need action. If they are bills, look carefully for any dates by which they need to be paid, and allow a week or so before the due date for posting first class. If cheques need to have cleared, work out NOW, the dates by which they need to be paid, and include 3 days minimum for posting first class (after all you may not get to the post box straight away!).

Write the date and what you need to do, clearly and boldly, on a sticker, post-it note or in a diary where you will obviously see it. Alternatively, put it in to the diary of your mobile or electronic calendar. Make a point of looking at this **each** day to get you to *ACT.*

Buy some first and second class stamps, envelopes and a box file or container to put all your bills into, with a section for letters and anything else of importance and without fail, always put things back into this file each time. (Don't leave things about, where they may become lost or moved!)

When you have completed the action or chore from the list, cross it out with a definite feeling of satisfaction. Acknowledge that you have not procrastinated at all but have dealt with it responsibly and in a timely fashion. Don't dismiss your achievements, but feel the pleasure of relief, and feel really entitled to chill out.

You can see that organisation is a key to ACTION.

Tip

As you make a start on the thing you know you must tackle, note what the time is. Say 11.30am—then think—if the job takes half an hour by 12 midday this job will be done. And know that by the time 12 midday arrives you have actually achieved the job. 12 will come anyway—and if you've not tackled it—it will still be 12 but *without any_accomplishment,* and you will still have the job to do. So, identify a time, knowing that by then it will be done and *you will be free.*

Now go back to the list.

The other things you have to do are still there although it would have been lovely if in the meantime they had disappeared, but that has not happened. However, sometimes they are less urgent. So find the next two things that are imminent, or important and highlight those to a post-it note, diary or mobile, with date of accomplishment.

When letters are received, you have the option of opening them immediately to see how important they are and if you can deal with them during the course of the day, or you can open them on return home and deal with them then. Add to your list, mark on a sticker, the date to deal with them, and put them into your folder or box file. Choose a time to go through your post and read what action is necessary. Make a note of phone numbers, emails, etc. and make the call.

People put off phoning because of all the information that is needed for automated calls, which normally require passwords and personal information. Have this at hand *before* you pick up the phone. However, when it is urgent, phone anyway and see how far you get. Don't assume that there will be difficulties, just find out.

You can always phone back.

Procrastination is born from a scenario which assumes all sorts of difficulties before even the first hurdle has been reached. Procrastination allows the mind to be filled with reasons why what you want to happen, won't happen.

Try this new word: ACTION. Call, write, communicate— *see* what happens.

Know things about ACTION. Firstly, you are doing it! Not thinking about doing it, not worrying about doing it, not imagining what will happen if it goes wrong. You are being courageous, you are finding out, you are helping yourself, you are being in control of events, you are initiating an outcome, you are trying your best, and if that's the case, no one can do better.

If you have to ask someone to do something for you, do not invite disaster by dreaming up all the reasons they may say no. Whether you believe it or not, just ask. You may get a no, but politely ask Why? Do not be afraid to ask. Do not be afraid to know the answer you *will* get, as opposed to worrying about the answer you *may* get. One is fantasy, the other is a place to move on from. Don't give up. Seek another avenue of enquiry. Ask someone who has had the experience. You don't have to take their advice. The ball is still in your court, but at least you have more information to go on with.

Know that it is your right to enquire, particularly if it is a service for which you are paying. It is expected and indeed you will be required to ask for help all through your life, so practice as much as you can—it becomes easier.

Take the responsibility for ACTION. Get out of your own way for keeping you stuck! This is your Right and your Burden. Nothing and no one can progress unless ACTION is taken. Be in control of the ACTIONS you make. You will have to re-act less, moving from scenarios which throw you into dilemma, as opposed to those you deal with effectively.

Initially you may find more actions attach themselves to your list. This is the flow of life finding expression— think of it as a creative outlet because it is giving you a chance to practice new methods, and, indeed, the flow inwards is clearing the backlog which you did at first allow to accumulate. But eventually you will be in control of a useful device called DISCIPLINE which enables you to tackle actions without thinking about what you need to do to achieve the outcome. You actually just do it.

Don't be afraid to list what you want to achieve, now and in life. Casting your thoughts into words allows direction to manifest, and soon you will find some of your hopes have a chance of becoming reality. Life does work that way. Without the knowledge of your aim, your life's energy cannot be channelled to a cause and can only go round and round bringing you the same life's experiences that you've already had.

Your destiny really wants to take you to the best parts, but needs to know from you where that is likely to be. It may not be a place, but an expression of life, or a feeling. Just express your desires on paper, capture the nebulous dreams, and let the miracles begin to initiate the new and exciting directions which *your life* can take. Suspend disbelief, or a negative reaction which appears to suggest impracticality, and let your thoughts take wings.

Just Do It! (Don't procrastinate!)

If you really can't go from Ditherer to Doer (Unreliable to Reliable) in one fell swoop, give this plan one good try at least. Learn from outcomes. Feel the sensation of worry (not doing), and the sensation of freedom (accomplishment). And if down the line, you become stuck, frustrated, at the mercy of inaction and its outcomes—try again. And Again. Because actually YOU are the only one who can take ACTION in your life. And YOU deserve to receive the best, if you DO THE BEST YOU CAN.

Negative intentions can only have Negative outcomes. Positive intentions allows for Positive outcomes, and even though they are unassured, their positive influence has a better chance of aiming nearer to the mark, which will get you closer to where you want to be.

So BE OPEN TO IDEAS, OPEN TO OPPORTUNITIES, TAKE ACTION and DO IT NOW!

COURAGE

Courage is usually associated with heroic deeds. Actions, which in the face of adversity, are forthright and brave.

But there is other courage. Day to day living courage. Courage which we all need. Courage which we all have inside ourselves, ready at our command to support our actions.

Courage is one of the powers within ourselves which is ready when we need it to support the decisions we take. Believe that Courage is there, inside yourself, ready to empower you in your choice of action.

As we awake each day, Courage is one of the fuels on full alert, ready to be exercised, raring to go. When unused, its fuel lines get a bit clogged. Caution, doubt, indecision halt its flow. But Courage is still there, its energy levels registering full, ready to assist you in achieving the actions which feel uncomfortable.

Courage is your best friend. The messenger which whispers in your ear "You can do it". Courage is the deep breath which propels you forward, closing the door on fear and doubts, enabling you to take the first step, or the next step, or the final step.

Friends can give you support, but Courage is your own source of power, and you need never doubt that it is there to serve you. Fear of outcomes and reactions stand in the way of progression and advancement, but Courage neutralises their effect whilst you achieve the accomplishment of a new and well over-due intention.

Consider the numerous times during a day when you need Courage.

It can even start as you make a move to get out of bed. What will the day bring? What will they say? How will I react? Today, I must tell that person adverse news. I haven't completed a piece of work on time, what will the outcome be? I am late. I no longer want this type of life. How will I cope? I need more money. My exams are today. I feel down.

Fear is often the first feeling we have on waking up. And it can pervade us all day long. Fear succeeds in closing us down; taking away opportunities, because its closest ally is Doubt. Fear and Doubt keep action stuck. Fear and Doubt fog our hopes and intentions. They quell the opportunities by smothering them with delay and indecision. What antidote to this? What possible way out? Courage.

Courage. With a deep inhalation of breath, breathe in Courage. Know that you were born with renewable energy sources, whose function is to supply your being with an everlasting fuel to enable it to Achieve and Potentialise.

Courage. It surrounds Fear and Doubt and suppresses their effect, whilst the action is taken.

You will need Courage, because the outcomes are unknown.

Fear and Doubt about an action will have already shown the worst scenario and endeavored to keep you stuck in a place where they can reign unchecked. They do not like Courage. Courage defeats their hold. Courage takes you beyond their grasp. Fear and Doubt have to reassemble their forces, they will make you feel uncomfortable again. But Courage is there, renewed now, because you have evoked it from slumber. Seeing its chance to perform, Courage is there to take the helm, direct the next steps, lead you bravely on towards a better outcome.

Know this: Courage supports right action.

If the action you need to take is in your best interests, then Courage will enhance your powers and protect you.

If it is wrong, harmful action you seek to take, Betrayal and Deceit will come to your assistance. They are close allies of Fear and Doubt.

During the day you will say many things, take many actions, avoid unpleasant situations if possible and move within your zone of familiar discomfort and, at its close, be disgruntled that you had not done things differently. You will not know that you could have called on Courage, and things would be different now.

For days and weeks, and even years, patterns of behaviour continue to circle. The circle appears to widen, but sometimes it just moves. Sometimes we are trapped with the behavior of colleagues, friends or loved-ones, in situations that we wish would change. We think about them. We hope for different outcomes. We perhaps try our best. We soothe, we help, we argue, we fear and doubt. And we perpetuate the life we know, albeit sincerely trying to make things different, or better, for us or for others.

If only we knew that Courage is there all the time, waiting for us to break out, make the move, create the intention into reality.

Courage needs to be called upon. It needs its summons to attend to the job in hand. All it needs is to be unlocked from its source within you, and it will show itself to be the powerful force in your life for change.

Now this is where Fear comes in again! Aha, it says, I can run this show. I know how to stop this individual progressing. Show him what could happen, show him the worst, keep him stuck. Fear can prolong a poor relationship for years. Fear can prevent a person progressing in a job. Fear can keep the bully bullying. Fear can stop you crossing the road, making a sound decision, making any decision, Fear makes indecision and confusion.

Courage seeks a strong way forward. Courage has Universal Help as its source. Courage helps new actions take place. Courage helps decisions to be made. Courage enables words to be spoken which clarify the situation and lead to better understanding between people. Simple needs require Courage to be present when they are requested. And if simple needs are denied, then Courage is required to try for a different approach, or outcome, or the rhetoric to change the course of the prevented action.

In the course of your life, your levels of Courage are always topped up to the full. Because you are always needing them. Each day.

To say the thing that needs to be said, needs Courage.

To take the action to make things better, needs Courage.

To finish a relationship. To start a relationship. To maintain a relationship.

To cross the road, climb the stairs, stop smoking, stop becoming drunk, start eating the right foods, start exercising, all actions require Courage.

Why? Because each action is a step into the unknown. Courage leads to Change. And Change can be scary. It means facing up to a different life, life-style, or partnership, or job, or even attainment of an intimate action which changes your partnership. But Courage comes with you in this new stage, and it has been freed from restraint, so its power is greater to enable your progress to be more easily achievable.

Courage has the most uplifting comrades: Hope, Optimism, Achievements, Faith, and a greater awareness of working towards a better life for yourself and those around you.

Give Courage a big chance in your life. Replace Fear and Doubt with Courage. They have had their big day, Make Courage the first player in your Life, and call upon it all the time to get you to do what you want to do for the best in your life.

Inhale Courage. Smile. Be light hearted, Courage hears your call. And is there for You.

DESPAIR

Welcome to my lair! You will arrive at the entrance when life has let you down. I always welcome weary, desperate, angry or battered souls to share my home. It's hard out there, I'm told.

Times are tough, everything is changing: you've lost something, or failed to gain what you most want. There seems little point in going on. I agree. I never leave. Which makes me the most reliable of ally's. If you need sympathy, you have come to the right place.

I not only understand where you are coming from, but with my help, where you can always stay. You don't have to try hard here. You can relax, let all your worries, concerns, broken dreams, hurts and frustrations fester here. I will gradually coax them out of you, day by day. It's the one place where if you arrive with little, you will gain more of what you've got. You just need to let all your sorrows flow out—don't mind us here, we all feel the same and can add to your list of failures and complaints—which are, of course, not your fault in any way.

The world out there is always trying to make you feel bad for the choices you made, when, of course, you didn't have a choice. It was their fault, I agree. I hear it all here, you are not alone. So many souls feel bad. They feel hurt, desperate and at the end of their tether. Here you will be among friends. In fact BLAME resides here when he's not out there garnering more souls to join us.

BLAME is amazing. Give him any situation and he will show you how there was no other choice to make except the one you did. He is a master at taking your power and responsibility, making you feel better and everyone else suffer. I expect you've already made his acquaintance though. Between you and me, I think he's a meddler. Without his insidious thought process, you may not have arrived here. So he is my friend—I am grateful for his efforts and he too will continue to be your friend during your stay here.

But don't stand out there hesitating, come on in. You've earned your place. It's warm and squelchy underfoot. No hard roads here to tackle, just a familiar place to unburden your load. You may never want to leave. I will show you just how hard life is out there and why you should stay with me.

Oh why is the door being locked? Well we don't want OPTIMISM and HOPE to get in. They cause chaos with the system and entice souls to leave. Here we are just one big unhappy family! What more could you want in life?

Oh sorry, you do want more in life? Well we will get to that later. Put it off until tomorrow— PROCRASTINATION will help you. Although he's on call all the while at the moment—no one out there seems to want to do anything *now*.

And you are asking about how long your stay will be. As long as you like—take your time, you've been through such a lot—there I go again stirring up the memories— oh I can see it could be a lengthy time (with my help!), so just wallow—you will soon believe my mantra that there is nothing more you can do, and that everything you've tried has been wrong. I'm not arguing! I see it your way!

Find a place to call home and curl up. Oh you've noticed there are no windows. Well why would you want to be reminded of life out there? Other rooms? Oh no—this is it. Some call it a dead end, but frankly why would you want to be alone when together we can endorse each other's need of sanctuary. Privacy and solitude entice you to look inward—that can't lead anywhere except back here, and you've already arrived so what good would introspection be. Enjoy this dark, warm place and I will make your stay increasingly pessimistic and drawn out.

What can you learn here? How hopeless and desperate your life is! I will assure you of all the negative, pessimistic thoughts you already have. You will not have to seek solutions; you will not have to think, you can just be—as miserable and sorry for yourself as you wish. All day long for as long as you like.

You may wish to leave? But why? After I've invited PESSIMISM and HOPELESSNESS to talk to you, there will be no reason you will find to want to go.

Okay—you're argumentative. You think you may want to leave! Ha! We can soon deal with that! WORRY get over here right now. This soul needs something to chew on, something to think about, and your devious means of diverting positive action is needed.

Have souls left? Well they've tried, but I normally reach out to pull them back from the brink of 'Trying Something Different'. Mostly the mire keeps their footsteps safely in my domain, and their frame of mind, which I have tried so hard to maintain in negativity, actually allows them to fail soon after trying so they are back again from time to time.

If they do escape, however, I can coil my snare around them and drag them back to my lair, at any time. UNCERTAINTY and FEAR are always lurking, whispering in the ears of those who have left, or have not yet partaken of my evil hospitality.

How do you leave? I'm not going to tell you that. I want you to stay. Those paragons of virtue, COMPASSION, MERCY, HOPE, and FORGIVENESS are not welcome at my door! You won't get POSITIVE ACTION and HELP here. I encourage DISASTER, MISERY, and BLAME.

I am the final step. I am the bedrock of disaster. I am DESPAIR the Lord of NEGATIVITY and BLAME.

CHANGE

CHANGE—Often a frightening concept, because the future is unknown.

CHANGE—Sometimes a welcome challenge to a dull routine.

CHANGE—Sometimes a break in routine which gives us space and time to assess ourselves, and then propels us onwards to the next new experience.

Certainly there is a daily occurrence of change in our lives, from the news, to the weather and most of it we take in our stride. Indeed we appear to take it in our stride because there appears to be no time to think about it. Whether we want it, whether we have an option about it, and whether it will make things better or worse for us. Change just seems to happen in our lives.

Unwelcome change brings stress and frustration, as in unexpected redundancy, or breakdown of relationships.

Planned change is a signal for better times ahead, with hope for the future and raised expectations.

Tackling change with less drama requires flexibility and a degree of optimism.

Accepting the change caused by other people or outside events, where a decision has already been made, sometimes appears easier to deal with than the change which is consciously initiated by ourselves. Indeed when a change is made for us over which we have little maneuverability, acceptance, at least initially, is our only option. However, resentment can set in, if a negotiation about the way the change is implemented has not been taken.

Before we perceive the need for change, we have probably hit our head against the brick wall many times; we have pleaded, argued, tried guilt trips and anything but Change, to secure a future that requires no further new action, and which allows us to be lazy, blaming others for their inadequacies, rather than facing our own short comings.

We have already come a long way if we are on the verge of making a change. It means that events in the past have been unsatisfactory for us, and we have realised that there is a need to change our actions or outlook for the time ahead. By the time we have decided to make a change the main stumbling block has already been overcome: PROCRASTINATION. We are on the verge of taking our responsibility for our own efforts. We have changed from a victim mentality to a positive action mentality. Well done! So far, so good.

It doesn't mean we will never again revisit old ways, nor wander down the paths of old thinking, but it does mean we *intend* to do better, and that intention is very powerful at the time. To maintain the change is now the challenge. Use all the tools at your disposal: reminders, acknowledgement of improvements in one's self, or situations, feeling of empowerment, renewed confidence, new opportunities coming your way, rewards. You will need to keep acknowledging the change you have made, because temptations will be there to test your resolve and beckon you back to lazy old ways that didn't work in the past. Don't give in. Use your intellect to protect your resolve to keep to the new behavior. Keep going forward and give the Change you have decided to take, a blooming good try. Don't let it be sabotaged by anyone or anything.

Conscious change normally brings about better outcomes than we have previously experienced because we have decided to take right action. We have seen what is, and want what can be. Our Intention to proceed with right action has gone ahead and prepared the way, so that when we carry out the action, the way is less difficult for us to manage.

There may still be difficulties, upsets, hurts, arguments and disagreements to overcome in any relationship which Change affects, but now we know we are doing better than before, taking responsibility for our own selves, rather than seeking to change another's behaviour. Change that is experienced by ourselves and others is viewed as strength. Sometimes, even people close to us, dislike this strength. Perhaps it shows up their weaknesses, or fears as to what the future will hold, but keep right on. Change for the better will eventually bring better outcomes to everyone.

When deciding to change something, list the options, pro and con. What you will gain, what others will gain, who will lose out, what the change will mean, how it will work. State your intended change as clearly as possible—certainly to yourself, and if relevant to the person they will affect. Try to get as clear a picture as possible of what is keeping you stuck at present, and why this change is necessary. Don't be afraid to explore all the options in a situation. This can be a stumbling block, because we don't always want to see all the failures or faults in a situation, thereby admitting we are responsible for some of them! But this acknowledgement reinforces the case for change, and shows us what alternatives there are. Hence our decisions are clearer, more purposeful and relevant. And less easily undermined when scrutinized by a saboteur!

You will need to be positive, with hope or belief that the future will be better.

You will need to inwardly acknowledge the change and outwardly demonstrate the change. Have Courage. Know that you are being as wise as you can be at the present time. Practiced behaviour takes time: unlike bad behaviour, good actions require patience and time to manifest. And you are choosing to do something different for the betterment of your life and progress (career, relationship, mental attitude or new habit).

Have Courage to take the first step in the right direction. Know that new doors open when you make a change for the better.

Step 1   Intend to Change

Step 2   List the pros and cons

Step 3   Decide on the best outcome and best action forward

Step 4   Consciously acknowledge that what you are doing is for the best outcome and as kind as possible to anyone who may be affected by your actions

Step 5   Make the Change

Step 6   Reinforce your actions positively by affirmations:

I am making progress in the right direction.

I am taking responsibility for my actions and carrying out the changes necessary in the best way.

I am changing and life is responding positively to the change in me.

COMMUNICATION

How can we resolve the difficulties and faults in our Communication?

Often what we regard as communication is no more than a need to express what is on our mind, simply by emptying it of the thoughts we have been able to put into words. Because there are thousands of thoughts that happen simultaneously we are not able to succinctly put them into words in the time available. So what comes out is a fraction of the picture.

However what we term 'communication' in allowing our voices to be heard, is an attempt to be concise and we believe, accurate to either our feelings, or knowledge or logic.

Speech can be offensive by the way it is expressed. Our words are coloured by tone and emotions; by sarcasm, wit or sympathy. "I really need this" as an example. Said with desire "I really *need* this", or said with personal emphasis "*I*" really need this, or said with sarcasm "I really need *this*", or with sincerity "I *really* need this". The same words said with different emphasis and hence, different meaning. The choice of intonation comes from the communicator who thinks he knows what he means, and the meaning he is giving out.

Speech is complex, its nuances powerful—actual meaning is often muddled with inferred meaning— and it is all too easy for the deliverer to say something offensively, leaving the recipient reeling. No wonder our communication becomes confused.

To understand and unravel this complexity of the responsibility of speech, it takes time to analyse what happens with an intent to change the delivery in the future so that the same pattern of conversation does not occur, if we want to avoid upset, disharmony and prolonged arguing.

The person who is being spoken to will firstly hear the tone in which the words are delivered: a pleasant voice of level pitch or a sarcastic, bored voice, which may not be delivering the message intended.

The words will often require a response. Which puts the receiver into a quandary—what to say in response; how to phrase a response without giving offence; how to answer the need in a factual, logical, or emotional way, depending on what he has understood.

Apart from not hearing properly, deliberately mishearing, not understanding fully, being inattentive, or uninterested, the communicatee, has to quickly formulate a response to a subject he may not know anything about, nor want to know anything about.

The communicator will believe it is his right to speak whenever the need arises, or when the opportunity arises. The communicator may be in a frame of mind for discussion, but perhaps not the 'right' frame of mind for what needs to be discussed, but may press ahead regardless, because of the need to express ideas.

The communicatee may be tired, fed up with other problems, dissatisfied with areas of his life, or just about coping himself, and not want to take on more information or suggestions. There may just be overload in the recipient's mind which cannot let in any more concepts at that time, or most of the time. (This needs to be addressed, however, when partners need to sort out differences).

Within fractions of a second, miraculous impulses are carried from the mind, brain, cells, all over the body, to the relevant thinking monitors to motivate speech, as well as its delivery in tone and vocabulary, according to our width of expression, knowledge of words and the closest meaning we can convey—*at that point in time.*

For one simple sentence to be born, millions of miraculous things are happening behind the scenes within seconds of our time, and to the person to whom we are communicating, physically and emotionally. We rely on these automatic functions to serve us faithfully and respond as our need arises. We access our huge memory banks with expectation, and frustration should they fail us. We take so much for granted with what we term communication, and yet we use this miracle every time we open our mouths to speak.

Yet, just as thoughts arise from somewhere to be expressed, the mechanism for expressing them is immediately available to us in voice and communication skills. How often do we assess the content, validity, accuracy, need and tone, of what we are about to say? Extremely rarely, if at all!

This immediate, miraculous, infinitely clever and responsive mechanism that we have been taught to use— the whole package for hearing, thought, interpretation, response and speech—serves us to the best of our current ability throughout our lives.

But do we seek to improve, modify or more effectively use this modus operandi for BETTER, CLEARER, MORE PRECISE communication—very rarely!

The actual physical operations of thought, mental activity and speech happen so automatically, and could be likened to a computer. We access something we do not understand and it performs clever actions for us. We do not have to understand how, but use the tool according to our experience, and to the extent of our own investigation or knowledge of what it can do. So if we explore the computer further, we find other clever things it is capable of. But in order to do this, we have to invest time and thought and the experience gained is registered in our memory, so that the next time we use the facility, we use it better, quicker, more accurately and make connections we once never knew existed.

Liken the computer to the brain (or mind). A miraculous, God-given faculty which we each take for granted, which is transportable, powerful beyond our current knowledge, is a library of memory, interpretation, visual records, sounds, voices and *enables us* in every way to LIVE our lives—but is *underused*.

Even computers have updates, new monitors, protection by firewalls, new keyboards, text which can be modified, changed and deleted. So do our brains and total thinking and feeling mechanisms. These updates happen both automatically with cells being replaced and body parts automatically being renewed throughout life, and by the information we glean each day about our environment, or input from information picked up in books, newspapers, television (media).

Like a computer we need updates, modifications, health checks and protection from unwanted input, to accomplish the boundary breaking capabilities and spontaneous responses which our brain does deliver. As human beings, however, we do have the ability to tailor our minds to our own needs *if only we know how* this can be learnt and achieved.

Information we pick up and partially recall will be modifying our outlook, our interpretation of the world and our place in it. This peripheral information is useful to us to draw on, *but the real meaning is the script we write in life*. This is our focus—the point we actually want to make.

And to make this point we take breaks in our dialogue with the printed word, to review, think, focus, delete and add more information to clarify, stretch and incorporate more thoughts. So what we actually *say* is more focused and accurate than if words just tumbled out—and yet in communication with others, this is precisely just what happens.

Of course, quick thinking and speaking are very valuable and prized indicators of focused intellect, and where factual accuracy is required, or the ability to multi-task, or communicate with many and varied personalities, it gives the owners a decided advantage. To have the ability to hear clearly, understand the message, remember and recall what has been said, use this information for deed or word, translate back with meaningful response and make better future actions as a consequence of taking the best from the information given, is probably one of the best goals to achieve in effective communication.

But we can go further. We have learnt how to talk. We believe that is communication. But we can improve and break boundaries by using the whole package available to us. We can learn, from practice, new ways of accessing information already there, information we wish to retain, and information we wish to put out there—we can be informed; we can grow; we can become *good communicators*, not just mediocre talkers.

How we learn to talk: Babies are taught by word repetition, until the word begins to have meaning. The word is usually something visual, so that the meaning is attributed to something material. Then as the vocabulary extends, words showing movement are introduced: eating, moving, waving, clapping. Then words showing emotion: sad, happy, smiley, hurtful, loving. Words of colour, texture, warmth, cold—sensory words. Then concepts are linked together—Daddy home! Nanny gone! Me sorry! We learn to use words associated with our needs, comfort and immediate surroundings. Then, as our intellect grows and the world expands new meanings and expressions are needed and learnt.

There seems to come a time for many people, where the need to learn more is channeled into work or profession. Because the daily round does not offer the time to investigate other possibilities beyond what has to be done, the extra pressure of learning becomes a burden of necessity, and extra information can seem like overload. This is when it is important to begin or cultivate a hobby or interest unconnected to the conventional idea of learning, because *it is necessary to continually expand your knowledge.* New or different interests normally require expression, and this can prompt new ways of looking at things, different ways of tackling problems and usually more informed conversation.

We each need *new* input. It is the elixir of life. Our well-being needs expansion. We look for new ideas, new fashions, new music, new art, new countries to explore, new ways to decorate. We need to expand. And so does our conversation. The essence of what we talk about needs to be kept alive, to be interesting, entertaining, exciting and new. By motivating ourselves to expand our interests and knowledge we loosen the grip of inertia and become more inspiring, more inspired, more alive. By saying I will read more, learn more, take part more in life and activities, your very own being seeks expression. The part of you which is locked in, held down, fighting to be heard, will be heard! People will look to you for your input. People will turn to you for your knowledge and opinion on topics. *You will begin to become who you really are.* And your conversation will be *Communication.*

Think about *talking.* Think about what you say, how you say it, the content of what you talk about, the words you mainly use, whether you butt-in with comments.

Then think about *communication.* How you get ideas across. How you bring in new ideas to the conversation. How you listen. Whether you allow the other person to finish what they are saying. Do you use new words? Do you sound sarcastic, happy, boring, tired. What impression does your voice convey? Do you want it to convey that message? How much do you say? Do you ask questions? How do you respond to questions? If you give an answer, is it quick and short, or prolonged and complicated? Do you feel satisfied with your input? If someone else has good ideas, do you encourage them with supportive words? Do you put yourself in the other person's shoes, try to see life from their perspective? Do you think about what has been said after the conversation?

Conversation is an art. It can be a very reassuring and kind way of interacting with another person. It can bring comfort. Conversation is an exchange of ideas, facts, feelings, sympathies and encouragement. A real conversation, where both sides are heard, and discussed, can bring about a change for the better, and at the least, a better knowledge of how the other person feels, where they want to go, even their commitment to the relationship, and what steps to take next.

Conversation can be fun. In striving to improve the exchange of ideas, fun and laughter should be included in! A sense of humour builds lightness into the conversation, and it allows the less known side of a person to shine through. It also shows intellect— an obtuse way of making a point. Certainly when conversations get heavy and emotionally charged, a good way to diffuse some of the heaviness is to lighten up with a smile or a loving word.

So having spoken briefly about what conversation can be, and very briefly the transformation of thoughts into words, *How can we resolve the difficulties and faults in our communication?*

A structured approach may be needed:

Something isn't working—a communication that runs round and round, many times over many days, months and even years, or simply a conversation that became emotive over a few thoughtless or ill-timed words.

Myth—" a time needs to be set aside." In practicality this will not work. When the time arrives, partners may be involved with some other needful project, family may be in earshot, they may be happy and you do not wish to risk spoiling the pleasant times, and all the things that needed to be said at the time will be forgotten, muddled or lack conviction.

That is why improved conversation needs to be worked on as it will help heal situations before they become too big to handle effectively

The time needs to be immediately to discuss what isn't working. This in itself causes problems, just finding a time when one or both people aren't tired, lacking energy, not pulled in another direction by work, or family needs, or by doing the hundreds of things necessary in everyday life. A mutual time must be found for discussion—or simple easy conversation. This can be the hardest part of communication—finding the right time to speak, and indeed to consider what needs to be said, and done. Most often discussion arises at the most inappropriate time and is held amid a background of other activities and commitments, so that appropriate, needed and clear thought cannot be given to what needs to be discussed. But a right time for discussion seems to bring up a reluctance to do just that, because old injustices and scenarios are brought to the fore, that had poor and emotional outcomes, and the great reluctance to put oneself through the same tortures, is very often the reason why time is not allocated to discuss what is not working!

No one said it would be easy! But it is *necessary*—to avoid further repetition, to improve a situation, to gain reassurance of direction, to go through the hurt and come out the other side more closely bonded, or with the knowledge of parting ways.

Once conversation is under way, unhelpful and deliberately damaging routes of expression usually come into play. Old recriminations, things left unsaid, old hurts that haven't gone away, feelings of inadequacy, inferiority, hurt pride—all the emotions from the bottomless pit rise to sabotage the well intentioned discussion. And if we are not careful, instead of a two-sided, caring conversation, a battle ground is established, where little headway is made, but more wounds are inflicted and received. So these guidelines may help (here's hoping!).

Before raising a topic for discussion—take time out to think about it.

Think, and really define one problem. There may be many. List them. One word for each problem. Think what the problem is. Think of your part in it. Think of your partner's part in it. Think about what hurts you in relation to this problem. Think about what hurts your partner in this problem. Think how you behave when this problem arises. Think what you are prepared to do to change your behaviour towards this problem. Think how you could help to solve this problem. Think of your partner's behaviour to the problem, and what he could do to tackle it. Is it more of a problem for you, or him. So far you are *thinking*. This precedes action. Emotions will be rising. Scenarios played out, even without you both taking part. See how emotional you are. See how hurt you are, see how you need to make your partner understand how you feel, and why you do not want to repeat this problem. You are still just *thinking,* but you are also *feeling.*

Your own feelings are hurting you. Your partner has done or said nothing yet in this new scenario, just yourself, and yet your own feelings are intent on destroying your own happiness and fulfilment. So realise that when you begin discussing a problem, your own internal processes, which feel indignant, already condemn yourself and your partner. And *still you are just thinking!!!!*

Now, taking a deep breath and trying to regain some control over your run away thoughts, just be. Breathe deeply. Walk about. Drink something good for you (not alcohol!). Shake your body. Let the tensions caused by the emotions find an outlet (this could take a while) and think *release, letting go, clearing out, calm.* When some of your emotional release has taken place, reassess how you feel. Immediately, you may not feel a whole lot better, depleted, ravaged, or lighter depending on the extent and types of feelings you experienced. But later, when you are on more of an even keel, *think* again about the problem you wish to discuss. Go through the steps again. You may be more fearful this time, if emotions were brought up which caused distress. But as objectively as you can, go through a second time the list of problems, or the one problem, and see if you feel or think differently about it. You may need to do this a few times.

Remember that your partner may not or will not have had the same chance as you to be as prepared for the discussion. Don't expect he will have all the answers, or be willing to listen, or know what to say, or even want to hear what you have got to say. You could ask him to do the same format prep listed above in order to clarify his thoughts for himself, before a discussion, but very often people are not open to instructional advice, so creative discussion takes its chance as it progresses. However, with the benefit of a more clear vision on your behalf, there is more chance of a better outcome than previously. Particularly if you try to remain calm. Emotions at this point are more likely to have a negative effect on discussion.

So use simple, short concepts to clearly demonstrate the problem.

Use few words.

Identify what the fault is

Say it

Discuss how both of you can be different and do the scenarios differently

Agree to learn to do the changes and DO IT.

CHANGE AND MOVE ON!!!

The most reassuring conversational closure must be: that I've heard what you've said. I've agreed or disagreed, I'm prepared to . . . . I'm not prepared to . . . . We are finding a solution—it exists—it takes both sides to implement. We can move on. We will do this . . . . We need *not* visit this scenario again, because things will be different. I am making a commitment to change my behaviour. I wish/I do not wish to change me. I apologise for the actions that caused you pain. I love you.

THE MIND

Does it control us—or do we control it?

What is it? Is it a computer? Does it need maintenance, updates, or even to be unplugged?

It appears to control our thought and actions.

Indeed the mind is thought—but much more.

Everything we do, say, interpret, react to, appears to begin in the mind; and further, once the thought is there, any action we take is directed by more thoughts to progress it.

Memory is thought, of course—thoughts which are plucked from myriads to connect and create a past scenario, set in stone (or ether) so that we can remember the events of the memory.

But what is behind the mechanism which brings up thought?

Memory sometimes appears to work like a filing cabinet, sorting through files until at last, what was sought is found. But what puts those workings into action?

Each thought has a word-equivalent to relate to it. Does that mean that without words, we would not think!

If a table, for example, did not have that name, nor any other name, then would it not arise in the mind as an object? It would because it can be seen. It is solid (well, that's not quite true), but the word 'table' in itself brings to 'mind' a picture representative of many different types and styles of table. We zero in on the one we mean by a process of selection defined by further description, but what makes us recall the actual one in our memory?

Something is behind the actual process of thought selection. Is this the 'mind' then?

What is it?

We know what it can do (to a limited extent).

"It" can select thoughts. Analyse thoughts. Cause reactions. Cause actions. Select images, and incredibly create new, unknown, unproven ideas and the means for investigation and invention.

So perhaps the mind is where the synthesis of conscious and unconscious thought is woven together to give us our personal ideas about the world and our place in it.

I refer to conscious mind as the myriad things that our tangible senses relate to us—things we see, hear, feel, touch, smell and therefore class as factual; borne out by the knowledge that other people have similar experiences, so that they must exist. They are 'objective' if you like. Inanimate. Structured. Irrefutable. Solid.

Whereas subconscious thoughts, ideas, concepts, inventions and vistas appear to be 'subjective' (ie modified by shades of colour, density, 'personal' discrimination) and consequently far harder to define precisely or at all, because our human form (at its present stage of evolution), has only allowed our 'knowledge' to be expressed by words.

The 'ether' in which our subconscious thoughts live is as real to them as the air which we need to sustain life. And the two (if not more) areas of 'mind'— conscious and subconscious—make up the unit which is our individuality—our uniqueness in this world. Their synthesis is how we actually 'live'.

I believe that there are also many other layers of 'mind' for which knowledge, discovery and words have not yet been invented—which influence and direct our choices of thought and action. And that Power of all states of being and interpretation which governs every living thing and every etheric, auric, spiritual, subconscious depth of mind and matter, remains a mystery.

Man's egotistical intelligence which is limited despite its many 'discoveries', believe ALL will be revealed at some point in time. It will not—because as human-beings we could not cope with the overwhelming magnitude of <u>all</u> knowledge, <u>all</u> power, everything revealed. So remember, that what scientists go to lengths to prove is already there, waiting to be <u>un</u>covered, when the time and precedent are in place for its revealing!

Present time is the only short span in which new experiences are born. To go over what was (our remembered history of this life time), or came with us (if you can accept the premise for reincarnation), is unnecessary because there is nothing we can change about it.

But we are given the means needed to cope with the situations of this life time. What we may have previously endured is forgotten or unknown for a purpose—to let us live less burdened in this life. The only use in reviewing our past history is if a pattern quickly emerged (from this life-time) it would put us in a position to effect a change for the future. We could begin to direct our destiny to a more favourable direction. And only to that extent is time valuably spent reviewing the past. Apportioning blame, either to ourselves or others, is a waste of time and resources. Only learning and moving on with the aim of improving ourselves—personal responsibility—is the best use of precious time.

Along with the subconscious and conscious mind, there is the directing 'ether'/energy that surrounds us—strangely connecting us to each other at times. The collective consciousness which causes ideas to emerge at a particular time in different parts of the world, or closer to home, when coincidentally two people say the same thing together. Isn't that uncanny?

Mind, looked at like this, appears to be a mesh of filters which is the instrument and musician, the implement and the implementer, to enable fruition of output.

From where thought impulses come is still a mystery and perhaps it always will be.

Given that as humans we are bundles of energy, and each of our tiny cells has innate intelligence, then our impulses of energetic intelligence contribute to a field of energy around and within each of us. The energetic field guides, controls, aids and channels our human progression for a purpose unknown to us, shrouded in mystery, known only to the Ultimate Organising Power—God. Human society is working out to a plan of evolution, perpetuated by varied, innumerable computations and patterns.

And in the whole of this 'soup' we exist, with the potential for very individual lives, expressing unique thoughts, actions and inventions. Could this help to explain how each of us, our 'uniqueness', contributes to the whole by bringing everything we are into existence and so expressing life. In this way we really are children of God—or at the very least, amazing individuals!

So the mystery of 'from where' do our thoughts arise, is difficult to fathom, even though we are free to investigate/ponder and put forth 'ideas'. Human evolution seems to have progressed quite a way forward with ideas and technology in daily life. Because of scientific advances we believe we are the cleverest and most advanced of our predecessors. But we are a long way from the evolution set for our potential as a human race, on a planet which has the possibility of supporting life (if we are careful enough) for as long as we need to be here, in this human form—unless of course, our destruction as a race is also part of a master plan in the spiral of life in all its forms.

Refocussing on the topic The Mind. You see how easy it is to digress! Given a pen in hand, paper and time, the mind wants to spill its thoughts out into concrete form to be preserved or captured—and this 'spout' of ideas comes from thoughts which didn't know they were there until the focus and channel presented themselves. (So get writing I say!!)

Which in a very roundabout way makes you think 'what' prompted mind to release these thoughts—or create them in the first instance.

Well it must be acknowledged that of course we all live in an ocean of form. Ideas are continually being made from peripheral vision as well as focussed intent. From everyday objects, comments, information, computers, radios, television, books, schools, people, etc. a constant input of images and thought associations through which we accumulate input to a centre where they are made sense of, ordered, stored and attached to sensory information—smell, noise, feel, heat, cold—and influenced by the 'sense' of emotion—sorrow, joy, fear, anger, pleasure etc.

According to our individuality, these sensory feelings influence us to a greater or lesser degree. It is not a responsibility over which we appear to have too much control. Hormones, chemicals, pollutants, stimulants, nature, machinery, work place, town or city etc., as well as people we spend time with—happy, sad, struggling, successful, all have influence on our mental states.

Sorting through ALL the combinations in order to change what we want to put right, is such a huge task, that some special help is needed. Faith evolved because of mankind's struggle and the belief that God can and does orchestrate miracles. But we have personal responsibility for our part and can effect changes of some of the influencers—job, food, people we spend time with, space we give ourselves, things we focus on, exercise etc.

To bring a *better balance to any unbalanced emotional state of mind* there are various things we can do to make the best opportunity for the best outcome. The mix may need to be adjusted from time to time, requiring tweeking, as we change through the whole gamut of human existence—growing, declining, brightening, despondency, cheerfulness, health, fitness. The fine line of well mental health is a precarious balance of changing influences. And each of us copes differently with similar problems, according to our personal mind set, capabilities and knowledge.

But in spite of all this, we can positively influence how we handle our lives. We can influence the direction we are aimed in, and when we don't know where we are headed, we can do our very best at every opportunity to make a best outcome of the situation we are in.

We can know that everything is for a purpose, even if the purpose is unknown to us, and that the lessons we learn along the way work out something we needed to know, particularly if we move on from the problems, rather than repeat them.

Nature will ensure we do what we must do to become who we are meant to be. And this will be for the best reason, even if we do not see it at that time.

God or the Great Power behind All Life is around us all the time, whether we acknowledge it or not. You can call upon this Power at any time, and believe that even in the darkest moments you are not alone. Something beyond us all wants us to exist in order to try to fulfil the potential for which we were created.

Practical Ideas for giving direction to your Mind

Ideas, visions, feelings, compulsions, inspiration, thoughts—are all expressed by words. Surround yourself with *nourishing* words. Words that encourage, uplift life, help and take away fear and guilt.

You would not eat fruit that is rotten or meat that is off. You would throw it in the bin, dispose of it, rid yourself of it. *So do not hold on to thoughts* which conspire to make you feel unsafe, unsure and fearful.

As they arise, recognise these negative, unhelpful thoughts as destructive, upsetting and harmful—as poisonous to your mind (and body) as rotten food. And *REFUSE* to let these dark thoughts spiral in your mind, leading you to spend time contemplating them.

Fight them.

Refuse them your energy and time.

Sever your connection to them.

Visualise negative thought coming towards you and see it caught in a strong, gossamer net from which nothing can escape. It is taken up to the light of the sky, getting smaller and smaller as it recedes to a place where the energy is transformed into a positive atmosphere. Try to see transformation rather than destruction. (Energy cannot be destroyed, but it can be transformed—and this is kinder on the atmospheric environment too!)

Physically remove yourself to another location (from where these thoughts have invaded) and do something physical or useful or creative. You will probably not feel like singing or dancing, but do it anyway! Or *Punch a pillow.*

Know that your thoughts are always trying to find an outlet because they have energy so rather than keeping them stuck in a loop inside your body and head, find a safe outlet to allow the energy to flow out of you. Hit a pillow or buy a punch ball and let out the anger, pain, guilt and sadness.

Feel the pent-up, stuck energy of misguided thoughts leave you physically with each strike of the pillow/punch ball. When you feel exhausted, recognise the space you've cleared. If you feel sad or tearful, know that your body is forcing a path inside you so that your mind has a channel for expression, and visualise it filling with light. Mentally send a stream of white light into the place to be healed.

Repeat this visualisation whenever it is necessary.

Note about Light:

Light is appropriate in healing because it contains all colours, and energy vibrates at different frequencies depending on the colour band. So colour healing can be appropriate too. Metaphysically as well as physically, light allows us to see and to experience more. It opens the doors of the mind, and heals our hurts and pains. It clears out dark crevices and brings us alive and well. Many of the affirmations that follow may be appropriate: Said in the present tense, choose one or two that appeal to you and repeat them as often as you like—they will bring a sense of balance and healing.

I am allowing light into the dark crevasses of my mind.

I am sending the messages from my mind to the light to be transformed.

The turmoil in my mind is being bathed in light, transforming it to positive good energy for my well-being.

I am allowing light to bathe my mind in peace.

Light is hoovering up the debris in my mind, disposing it away from me, where nature will transform its energy for my good.

Amidst the anguish, God is with me/The Power is with me.

I am safe. I am strong. I am being healed and made whole.

I am capable. I deserve the best life I can live.

I am in control.

I choose to believe that I am a worthy/loving/valuable and beautiful human being with some faults, but with aspirations to attain a happy and fulfilling life.

I am overcoming the deceptions of my complicated mind. God/The Power is helping me.

I dare to be very brave. I dare to exist as whole as I can be at the time.

Affirmations work because their positive messages, when repeated, are absorbed into your mind where they work to reprogram inner dialogue for positive results (overcoming negative thoughts which spiral downward).

Make your affirmations in the present tense (because action is happening now, not in the past or future). Write them on post-its around the home or car.

If during a crisis you feel over-whelmed with grief, *know* it will not go on forever (even if you fear it will at the time). You will come out the other side. Life itself wants you to exist and forces around you want you to succeed to live another day. So however bad it all feels, sever the thoughts that bid you 'give up' or 'it's no good' or 'it doesn't work.

Affirm.
I am healing the turmoil inside.

I am safe and I am protected.

Thoughts that fight each other are really striving to be heard—each wishes to dominate the other. The true YOU will eventually be able to discriminate any wisdom and discern what is useful and what is not. For now, aim to silence the overwhelming clamour which demands your attention and firmly say NO.

For a more prolonged state of calm, peace within and assurance that your worst fears do not become reality, a balance needs to be established. A sort of line from which you can wander from time to time from elation to despair, but come back to—for health and sanity. We really do not cross the line as easily as we may imagine. For life wants to nurture us, and has far more use for a soul who wishes and is trying to transcend life's darkness. A line is an illusory means of describing a boundary, but in the Thought World boundaries are gradual and moving outward, to accommodate the extent of human exploration. So when you may feel you are at the edge, in fact it is only a darker space you enter, where unseen hands help you back into the light of life.

Balance isn't really a thin space defined by right and wrong. Balance is a continual flow within wide parameters between which we experience a range of human emotions and constraints. Balance requires extremes so that the mid-range can be found. And it is here, in the mid-range that rationality serves us best, and because of the comfort here, this is where we try to head home to. But it really doesn't mean that we need to live without causing a few ripples here and there! We are always trying to push boundaries one way or another; it is what life appears to be about. But near the edge we are less well equipped to deal with unknowns, so balance for the most part of life seems to be a good place to head towards.

Good, positive thoughts make us strong. Deny air-time to any thoughts which take away your power.

Engage your body to let it help you overcome the destructiveness of your thoughts.

Stamp your feet. Wave your arms widely. Jump up and down. Release your demons!

Things inside us need expression at different times of our lives. When things we desire, need or want are denied us, the 'energy' of the desire still remains. It gets stuck and like dirt in a corner it doesn't go unless it is hoovered up or brushed out. And like dirt it is reluctant, and doesn't give in without a real scrub. It takes effort. It takes time.

In all the recesses of our minds, energy is stuck—either as unfulfilled desires or aspirations waiting to be released (the normal human condition!). This energy appears to be manageable because we chip away in small ways at its vast potential, appeasing its murmurs to be heard and acted on.

But when a crisis time in our lives appears, it is the whole body and mind crying out to be heard. And its message is exaggerated, furious, all-consuming and very scary. *'I'll show you!'* say the unbidden, hurtful, cruel thoughts. And it does, and how! Its idea is to scare you into submission; to abandon hopes of a 'back to normal' feel. Because basically the mind/body experience doesn't want you 'back to normal'. It wants you changed. It wants you to know that 'it' can't cope and that you need to take charge.

During crisis we become fragmented, cut off from other parts, incomplete, dominated by one force bigger than the others. Our mind becomes the master demon, dreaming up all manner of possibilities, likelihoods, potential outcomes, more and more obscure and ridiculous than previously (though seemingly real). Where these thoughts come from and how they arise, or even why, appears to be an interesting, all-consuming dilemma to be contemplated at any spare moment. Such is the mind's capacity to subterfuge your best intentions to switch off and control it. The possibilities for exploration are innumerable and fascinating, taking up your time and energy, but in the end *get you nowhere useful*. So just don't go there! (Put aside this study for sometime in the future when you can be distanced enough not to be involved in the situation).Otherwise you will become entangled in a web of spiralling thought—not having moved forward at all.

The point about becoming fragmented is that it is a state of mind which is crying out to be *united* with the whole of you. All the other parts of you still exist, but this one part takes centre stage for a time, appearing to become larger than all the other parts. But this is just an illusion and when it's had it's say, it re-joins the other parts of what makes you—your body, your life, home, job, friends, etc. and that is what sees you through—that you become a total entity again (even if you like some parts better than others!)

The ego is really giving you a chance to step in and take control. To master the new skill of doing *what's best for you.* 'You' have to take control. You have to act. You have to find the best way and only YOU can do that. Others can help, offer guidance, and be there for you—but only YOU can take positive action in your own life—you come with responsibility as a human being—and yes, it is difficult.

You will notice when all the thoughts which over-powered you, suffocated the real you, with their graphic imaginations, are less intense because you are gradually taking positive control of your mind (which for so long has been undisciplined). The stronger you have been in life, the quicker and more successful your healing will be. But anyone who starts to take control for the thoughts they allow to occupy their minds, is afforded help from unseen powers. The aim to move into a more positive frame of mind and deed is willed by life itself, in order to 'balance' the negative forces which surround humanity.

Choose to do something creative—then your mind has a respite whilst it concentrates on what it is currently trying to achieve and undesirable thoughts can be blocked out better. Drawing/writing/singing/dancing/ keep fit (in the privacy of your home if you prefer) gives a lovely feeling of freeing up, alignment, strength, and happy energy. Do it. See how your body moves—freeing your inner spirit and sensual self.

So here you are, needing to move forward. But the dilemma is that the best intention during a 'good' period becomes less urgent, until the overwhelming distractions of an undisciplined brain sends out messages which appear to be difficult to control. The thoughts seem to come unbidden, floating into the mind, taking us unawares. A sudden brain-storm of the scariest kind, makes us believe in the *possibility* (but note: not the probability!) of some wrong action. The imaginary line within each of us, which seems to represent normality, appears to be crossed and all the definite understanding becomes indistinct, unnerving us, hindering our abilities to be logical; undermining our confidence to make decisions; any decisions; the right ones. The crisis point is when we don't know ourselves, who we are, why we do what we do and what is required of us. An empty chasm to be crossed from one side to the other.

At these crucial, lonely, frightening times, no words of wisdom, no good intentions, nor people around us, nor phone calls, even seem to matter, let alone do any good. We are alone. We are made to face the situation we are in. We did not ask for it, mean it to happen or wish to bear it. But this last thing is what we must do: *Bear it.* We must learn from the experience of the pain of isolation that on our own is the only place possible at this particular time. We will manage to get through it. It may appear to teach us fear, but it will really teach us strength. Because when the crisis subdues (and it will), you will still by 'You', alive and stronger. And what happened in your mind, happened there—not outside you. Not in the world around you, but *within* you. As horrible and truly fearful as it is—your mind will have won on your behalf.

When we are going through the intense, overwhelming period of crisis alone, nothing seems to reach us. We may want to be held, shielded, helped, but the well worn ruts down which our mind seems to funnel, allows no passageway for comfort. But courage answers the call, for it is motivated when most needed, by life's desire to survive, and so we do—and we can live life differently from now on. (Each time!).

During a time of crisis, try to visualise something strong and significant to concentrate on. For example, a strong red letter **H** (suggesting structure, firmness, strength and balance) or any other image which is positive, clear and uncomplicated, and which comes to mind instantly. Look at the symbol in your mind from all angles— follow its contours, concentrate on it in the midst of your imaginings and it could help you to get through your crisis. The symbol will be a focus, stabilizing your mind and holding it fast, whilst the thoughts swirl around. It would be both an anchor, and a float for your 'being' helping you to come through the situation, with you more in control.

All the above takes practice, hence a meditation class, or learning visualisations and affirmations practiced when you are in between times, which will help your mind to become strong, healthy and able to choose what it will allow itself to be filled with.

Because after all—*we can choose what we will allow our minds to take in. We can select and discriminate.*

Most of us don't because we never think about it! We haven't been taught that it is possible. And we haven't been taught how. But we can learn. And that is what we should do! How to *use our minds and brains* should be No 1 priority for the whole of mankind—because we have so much more potential than we will ever know.

List problems and solutions

Sometimes it can be difficult to list problems and solutions and this may not be an appropriate time, but you could include the questions below in order to clarify your current position and where you want to get to.

A plan of Action:

Make lists of what you want to achieve:

a)   in life

b)   in overcoming this present dilemma

c)   what keeps you stuck

d)   do you want to move on? Why?

Don't forget—very importantly—what you are good at; what you like; what you dislike; your achievements and how beautiful you are, inside and out. Learn to love all of you—you really are worth it!

Also anything you can change to encourage a healthy body will be very useful, because if a body is in balance, this will assist the mind in coping. Alternative healing methods, including homeopathy, herbs, vitamins, crystals, light therapy amongst others, could be worth exploring.

> People are always around to help you, support
> and do the best they can for you, but . . .

> ACTION is yours alone to take

> Words motivate action, but you
> must implement the action,

> Your MIND will tell you which action to take.

LIVING

We live, but are we alive?

Living can be coping; managing different roles; doing all the things necessary to get us where we need to be—to work, to school, to the party. The numerous functions each of us has in relation to other people; our expectations of ourselves; the way we look, the responses we are expected to give; the jobs that need doing; the work that won't be done unless we do it; the people we need to comfort, talk to, remember, send information to; the articles we need to read. The list is endless, and this list becomes our function in life. Nothing else seems as important, so critical, as to keep doing what we perceive as important in life, when we really haven't had much time to give it any thought. To keep on; to maintain standards and expectations; to routinely do all the chores, to function.

And we do this without much thought, particularly when we are well. A person in good health can do all these things, and more, like the extra-curricular tasks that make up our leisure time—partying, sports, eating and drinking, being with friends. With good health, people do fill their lives to the brim. Time, after all is precious. Time goes quickly, and tasks need to be done, so fill each moment to cramming point in order to achieve.

There are times in our lives (times that stretch into years, particularly when families are growing up) which are consistently lived in this way, and we are grateful when we have the good health and energy to cope with the demands that appear to dominate the expression of our lives. We are appearing to manage, and this pattern sets itself up, so that life at a different pace is seen as a luxury, its place mostly at holiday times, when we give ourselves the permission to relax. And it is true that millions of us in the human race perform in just this way. (Is it really a human 'race'? Is an E missing—'humane' race?)

But a halt is called when people become ill. Many functions have to stop, however, 'driven' people still fit in as many of the ordinary functions as possible, fearful of what stopping may cause. Moderate ill-health is usually seen as an inconvenience, a frustration which won't allow us to function at the same hectic pace as we had been used to. With the same lack of attention as we gave true living, we now also can give ill health, lessening its hold by ploughing on regardless, continuing to neglect our bodies call for respite, feeling good about not giving in, not understanding the signals our bodies are giving us.

Consequently, sometimes, we are given BIG messages, to take a break, to reassess, to do life differently. A period of sick leave or recuperation can actually give us the time to rethink how we can run our lives to a slightly different tempo—and at least whilst the illness slows our responses, the change from rushing about does seem welcome, if annoying; but good intentions made at this time seem to have a habit of fading away, once full health and energy is regained, because nothing outside us has changed, except more tasks which haven't been dealt with, whilst we couldn't manage them! So life itself seems to have a way to perpetuate this frenzied, treadmill of existence.

Sometimes life is not running at full pace, more at an unchanging, regular pace, which is easier to manage perhaps, but lacks the excitement of challenge, through its repetition and predictability. Restrictions of job, money, time, and the circumstances of life in which we find ourselves, can cause frustration and a deadening of the senses, but there is little that can be done to change the circumstances, so life has to be endured. During the painful times, or during brief respites, such as holidays, or time out, people may seek a real change in direction, but again life itself seems to perpetuate the familiar way of life, which although frustrating at times, can be endured, and so it goes on.

MOTIVATION is the key to get life running differently.

Mostly there has to be a problem, a worry, a concern or something in life that is not happening happily, to actually get us to admit that a situation needs looking at.

So the first step is to look.

But looking takes time, skill and good judgment; so that the problem is not blown out of perspective, nor diminished. And it takes an ability to look at as many angles as possible—whose problem, why it has come about, is it livable? What and who would the changes affect? How many courses of action could be made available? Which courses of action would need to be taken.

Thoughts, left to circulate in the head, become more confused and tumble about in all directions, muddling the problem and adding to its size, kicking up associated emotions which magnify the dilemma. Far from being a catharsis, which consequently clears the problem, the muddled thoughts merely add fuel to an already simmering pot of mixed messages and emotions.

No wonder many of us give as little time as possible to making a solution which will lead to change. It is tiring, depressing, wearing work, even just looking, let alone putting anything in place, which is the next step.

A 'For and Against' List could be drawn up with written responses, so that the problem becomes clearer, or at least more visible

Hopefully having identified where an area of life is not working as well as it could, the choice becomes, can I live with this, or shall I set in motion some actions which will bring about a change? And that is if you have reached this point of enquiry. Many will have given up at the first hurdle.

It can feel easier to go on with the dilemma, despite its displeasure, than embark on actions which cause upheaval, use of energy, and disgruntlement where other people are involved, and which will cause a change in current circumstances, that have given a degree of comfort and security, for all the heart ache you have also gone through.

But here is where MOTIVATION comes in.

The very sight of the word is scary!

It means moving from where you are to the next place. Which indicates change. Which can be challenging, and fraught with the danger of the unknown.

Because the future is unknown, and the goal posts can easily be moved, you need to stay flexible to deal with future challenges as they arrive. Where you think you want to be may look quite different if and when you arrive there!

But MOTIVATION is the big M word. It is the vehicle that gets you from where you are to where you see yourself better placed, or think you want to be.

Motivation is keeping the goal in mind, whilst finding as many ways as possible to keep your outlook positive, keep your options open, but focused to the way you want to head.

Be aware that when you take a direction for your betterment, life will move you in that direction. There may be obstacles to test your resolve, which come up to be noticed and cleared, or to keep you stuck. Knowing you always have a choice may seem a useful bit of knowledge, but at this point it's only use will be a get out clause, which will take you back, not just to where you were, (because that will have changed), but further back to entrap you, so that making a decision for change in the future will be harder still. So basically, when you are making a change, know that there is no way back and that MOTIVATION IS MOVING YOU IN THE DIRECTION YOU WANT TO TAKE.

Motivation propels you forward. It is the fuel which kick starts your mind, when it is easier to procrastinate, waste time, keep in limbo, see what comes up, take no decision, leave decisions up to someone else, give away your power. Motivation makes you claim your power and the responsibilities that go with it. Motivation stands up for your right to change your circumstances and response to what life throws at you. Keep it at the forefront of your mind, and then try these exercises to see how Motivation fits you.

Right now—Relax. Wherever you are right now. Sit still, unclench any part of your body which feels rigid. Go around your body and try to sense where your muscles are tense, and just let go. Uncurl, unfurl, relax your face muscles, your mouth, your eyes. Go on. Just for a few moments. Remember to breathe, but not forcefully, just naturally for the moment. Whilst you are concentrating (and doing something consciously by going round your body, relaxing its various parts), you may be content to do just that. But when everything is relaxed, just notice how quickly your mind kicks in to take control: You can't waste time just being, doing nothing, just sitting, there are hundreds of things for you to get on with . . . yes we all have those messages at first. But recognise that you have given yourself permission to take time out. For a few moments you said 'Yes' to something you decided to do, for you, as an experiment in seeing where Motivation would lead you.

Ooops, did it lead to someone saying wake up, no sleeping on the job, or was that just in your own head. The controller in your mind does not want to lose control of you, and is quite happy that everyday life runs to a tight schedule without a spontaneous thought or break from routine. It makes its life a lot easier, not having to adapt and think up new ways of keeping you stuck. But just for a second or two you did take control. You regained the power of your mind to make a decision for YOUR GOOD.

Now try a second exercise.

You are rushing about, mind wise or bodily, thinking of the many things you are presently doing, or have to do when you get home, or next week, or for a meal, whatever. Now, immediately, just think one thought. Let it be a large, red capital M. Just see it. Follow the contours, see the strength of the shape, see a bright, vibrant red. Hear the sound M.

How long did your concentration last—two seconds? Well done! You took control and broke the pattern of consistent thought that inhabits your mind, closing out your will to think spontaneously.

Now decide for the third exercise to do this within the next hour.

Here comes failure. How do I know? Because with all the best intention in the world your mind is currently ruling all the decisions you think you make. And it has already decided to put obstacles in your way, during the next hour so that you can procrastinate for a good reason and not complete this third exercise. You can leave it for two hours, or do it next time you read this article, or you can let the knowledge that you failed, nag you until you decide to do the third exercise, and then have another change of mind, because something more relevant has come up! Yes, we know all the tricks, and we still allow them to take control.

Don't you ever get fed up with giving away the power of your mind to do what you decide?. Even now, you are probably thinking, this is not my idea anyway, you are making the suggestion, I don't have to do what you say, I am in control, I am not procrastinating.

But you are. You are making all the excuses possible to get yourself NOT to do what is good for you; which is to take control of your own mind.

So hopefully, your own wiser, stronger intention is to try this third exercise NOW!

Sit or stand still.

Close your eyes. Think of one concept—JOY.

Explore what it means to you. Other word associations with it, happiness, laughter, fun, smiling faces, love. Say Joy in your mind as often as you wish. See it written inside your head. Make it a bright colour. See how much you can associate with it.

Your thoughts no doubt will be wandering off down different paths. The tendency is to become annoyed that you could not focus for long at all, or you may even by unaware that your mind had wandered off (so long has it been used to doing just that, with no control from you). You will be tempted, even give up on this exercise as your mind whispers, it is a waste of precious time. You may open your eyes and say what is the point?. This isn't for me. I can't do this. I don't need or even want to do this.

Well just recognise that your mind is trying to control you, and this is exactly the type of procrastination that it excels at, in order to sabotage your intentions.

Congratulations, the exercise has been a success.

It has shown you why you have failed in the past, to ever get beyond good intentions. It has proved to you who is in control of your mind, and then your actions. It is not your conscious will that is currently in charge, it is your subconscious mind that runs the show—and pretty well too, for most of the time, but when you want to be MOTIVATED INTO A DIFFERENT DIRECTION, then you need to dominate your thought processes to work the way you want them to.

So going back to exercise three.

The Motivation is to get yourself, for three minutes, no more, no less, to control your thoughts sufficiently to think about an abstract concept which allows inspiration to raise your spirits, far from mundane thought. Think of a pleasing concept, a flower, sunshine, love, peace, sea, blue sky and enjoy the journey you will be taken on. Anything is permissible so long as it is NOT what you have to do next. If this happens, start again. Persevere for three minutes. If at the end of that time a battle has been raging, your mind has been fighting to hold on to the concept—again, although you will have failed to achieve what you set out to do, see how you have been tied to a will that is stronger than yours, and keeps you stuck. But now you know it, you have the power to control it, and the Motivation to do the exercise has won over your procrastination—so the exercise has been a success!

Tomorrow, when you try these 3 exercises again, you will not necessarily succeed. Success always comes when enough practice has achieved the desired goal. But these exercises are in Motivation—to get you to do what you want to do, even if it is for the smallest amount of time you will allow yourself to take. And understand that concept. You are the one defining how much time you spend on yourself, and on other tasks. You are the one, that actually says I am worthy of the luxury of time, I am able to take this precious time and make it something different, I am taking some time for myself, to relax, to work in pleasure, joy, laughter, I am taking some time to sit down and be quiet, and phew! This is the big one—I am taking time just to BE.

JUST TO BE? What does that mean? How can that be useful? It sounds like a waste of time! Surely I just am, when I am asleep. Why do I need time JUST TO BE? To be what?

It actually means to be still. To function consciously, aware, alert, still, and not be doing anything else at all. Not even fidgeting! To breath quietly, to sit or lie in relaxation, but not asleep or dozing. To allow the mind and body to be alive in a quiet, undemanding, peaceful consciousness—in a breathing space of absolute connection with All Life, but not Doing in it. Not moving, not worrying, not thinking constructively, but rather letting thoughts drift up and away. Just Being is connecting and allowing the force of life to flow through you, to nourish and aid your healing, and allow peace and balance to soothe you . . . .

Soon you will not be able to stay away. That will happen when you repeat the exercises a few times and find their achievement begins to get easier. You will want to be in the place where you can just BE.

Because you will feel better. You will feel calmer, more inspired, stronger and more able. Because you have given yourself the permission you need to take back the power of your control over what you allow your time to be used for. Along with all you have to do, will be the inclusion of what you want to do. And that will not just be five minutes with a gossipy magazine, where you remain passively engaged in some unrelated article that has done you no personally good service. But because you took Five, to reconnect with your Powerful Self, to give it expression and space and came back from the experience stronger and calmer and more rested.

Motivation has brought you here. It's not where you expected to come is it?

But the big M will always take you to a better place, if you are seeking the best life has in store for you.

And now taking a great leap Back to the Beginning—Life.

A way to inject 'Aliveness' into the daily grind, is to take back control over your thoughts and actions, to be motivated to Just BE as well as MOVE ON when necessary.

To BALANCE the BEING WITH THE DOING.

GIVING UP SMOKING

DO IT NOW!

There is no *best time*—there is only *procrastination*. Why procrastinate?

1) **PROCRASTINATION;:**

   a) allows us to get comfortable with an idea whilst we think about it

   b) allows us time to delay the right-action

   c) allows us to find excuses for *not* doing it

   d) keeps us stuck with an action within our comfort zone, with which we are familiar.

   e) says we really have little will-power, and prefer to be led, rather than lead.

2) **WHAT IS THERE TO FEAR?**

   a) The unknown. Without the habit, what will I be like? How will I handle the stressful situations my habit appears to help me with?

b) That I'll start giving up and then return to the habit and that would be a failure—I don't want to know that I could fail.

c) That friends and situations will coerce me into wanting to restart the situation and I will feel weak

d) That the change will be difficult, impossible or uncomfortable

e) That I will gain weight

f) That I will change

g) Having to be courageous and not knowing if I can be

h) Negative reactions from friends/peers

3) **WHAT IS THERE TO LOSE?**

a) ADDICTION

b) An exterior controlling force

c) Perceived immediate release from a seemingly overwhelming desire to smoke

4) **WHAT IS THERE TO GAIN?**

a) A higher level of good health for yourself—and for your loved ones

b) Increased wealth

c) Increased longevity potential

d) Feeling of power and control over one's own actions

e) Empowerment from the success of making a decision and seeing it through—knowing YOU CAN

5) WHY GIVE UP SMOKING?

a) Bad for health—asthma, clogged arteries, oxygen starvation to the brain, causing memory loss, breathing restrictions, years taken off your life

b) Waste of money (Add up a month's cost and realise what benefits this could be better spent on)

c) Potentially decreases fertility

c) Horrible smell of tobacco on your breath and clothes

d) Unacceptable socially

6) BEFORE GIVING UP SMOKING

a) List WHY YOU WANT TO

b) What the benefits are to you.

c) What better health you would have.

d) List the benefits to those closest to you, who care about you

e) Read information about smoking-related disorders and ill health, and put yourself in the imagined position of that ill health, and really see how irresponsible it is to continue the habit, knowing that you have caused the problem and cannot blame anyone else for your predicament. *Take responsibility for your life and the things in it you can control*

    f)   Understand that you are being responsible for effectively increasing your chances of premature death due to lung cancer and other related smoking disorders—that is what you are buying into when you buy cigarettes.

7) **WHEN YOU DECIDE TO GIVE UP SMOKING**

Congratulations! You have taken the first step!

NOW, today, the next time you reach for a cigarette just **DON'T**

Engage your <u>body to assist your mind</u>—this is very powerful.

You *can* control your hands! (Sit on them!)

Or, when reaching for a cigarette, imagine the packet full of boiling water and plunging your hands into the boiling water! The hesitating and withdrawal action, is the time you need to take control of the automatic reflex action and say **NO!**

You will be using your conscious mind to overcome the subconscious message that has taken up residence in a place where you should be in control—turf it out; use the eject button; force the messenger away who is playing havoc with your will power; see it as a destructive evil in your life and replace it with an image of you in control, you with the power. Destroy the silent voice that niggles at you. Think of it as interference which you *can* switch off.

Re-message your brain in this way and it will obey you! It has been asking for assistance for some years and you have ignored it—it is holding its ground but needs reinforcements—understand that your brain can be used like a computer; it responds to the information you give it! The subconscious is trying to work for you—create your major message with strong ideas in your conscious mind and you will accomplish what you need to do!

Imagine—we have this marvellous help at hand and very few of us ever use the tool we were born with to achieve success, power and control over ourselves! (Stupid—or what?)

Your determination, strength of will, belief that you can succeed are vital!

8) WHAT YOU CAN DO

    a) Make a chart of steps involved in smoking:

       —going into a shop to get your hands on a packet

       —taking out the money to buy cigarettes

       —handing over the money

       —taking the wrapping off and taking a cigarette out

       —putting it to your lips

       —inhaling

Be conscious of each action and know at any one point, you can stop the action. You are in control.

b) When you get out the money, and return it to your pocket instead of spending it—congratulate yourself.

If someone offers you a cigarette and you say NO, congratulate yourself. Really acknowledge that you are working with your inner self to deny the outer influence. It is so powerful to acknowledge each of the steps you make, so keep a list of tick points for each step you are successful in controlling and aim to make your chart as full of ticks as possible.

c) Don't buy any more cigarettes. Physically get out the money you would have spent on a packet and put it into a sealed, china money bank.

d) Take a cigarette and pull it to pieces. Spread out all the tobacco and as you pick up bits of it to throw in the bin—say:

You have no more hold over me

I hate the smell of you

I despise the hold you've had over me

I shut out my addiction to you

I am taking back my good health

I am taking back control of my body, mind and health

Your are no longer a part of my life—or my death

You make me physically sick

Repeat the message many times, with your fully determined mind, concentrating on the words, really absorbing the message—you are reprogramming your mind to help overcome your addiction. Once absorbed you will eventually have the means you need which will labour without your effort now that it knows how.

9) IF THE NICOTINE-NEED KICKS IN

a) Be prepared—have something else to suck, chew or eat. Do this slowly with concentration on the enjoyment of the alternative.

b) If you can, do some physical exercise—punch a bag to release tension, do some press ups, swing your arms from front to back and at circles in front, stamp your feet, shake your body. You are letting your body know that you are reinforcing its assistance to kick the habit. Your body will recognise your endeavours and increase its potential to help and work with enforced vigour to attain your goal. Your body wants to be whole; wants to be free; wants to serve you. Believe this and let it work for you.

c) Emphasise breathing out through pursed lips. Inhale deep breaths of fresh air through your nose. Enlist the aid of your lungs, to help them fight for their life with clean fresh air.

d) Have a hot bath to sweat the nicotine out of your system. Really see the brown stains coming out through all the pores of your skin whilst you relax in the hot water. See your body becoming clear and unclogged. Then shower to wash away the nicotine completely.

e) Imagine pure white air being drawn in to your body as you inhale through your nose. As you breathe in, see the white air rolling down inside your body to your lungs, filling you with a potent force with spreads to every cell of your being. See it absorbing the dark brown stains of the nicotine, pulling the nicotine into the white air, and as you breathe out through your mouth, allow the force of the exhalation to blow the nicotine away. Do this a number of times, to feel clean and lighter and freer. As the process renews and recharges your body, giving the cells space and brand new energy, you will feel more enlivened, relieved, courageous and stronger.

Bring your breathing back to a normal pace and know that although you may no longer be consciously controlling your breathing process, the programming of your mind is continuing. You have given your mind a new tool to help you succeed.

Your mind will work well because it is glad of your assistance in helping it fight the very addiction it has been reminding you to tackle! (SUCCESS!)

f) Say again the affirmations above.

g) Drink water or fruit juice

As you swallow this, again see it washing away the memory and harm of the nicotine, unclogging your system and cells, so that your concentration and thinking is clearer, sharper and focused.

10) SMOKING CREATES ITS OWN STRESS

You have reached for a cigarette because you feel stressed. The stress is partly caused by the way in which the smoke is cloying and clogging the cells by depositing tar, so that breathing is restricted, potentially causing headaches or pains which need relief. Drugs are used for the headaches; whist the cigarettes which have already overloaded the system, cause even more stress which leads to downward spiraling trend of ill health.

So you have reached for a cigarette because you feel stressed. You light up. You smell the familiar cloying choking fumes and without hesitation or thought, put the cigarette to your mouth, as though it had a will of its own! Once you inhale deeply to take the poisonous fumes into your lungs, surely you realise that you are causing yourself to die.

Trained with your careless consent, your hands apparently learnt such a familiar action, when you initially taught them, to take a lighted cigarette and put it into your lips and breathe down into your vital organs a poison which shortens your life, steals your will power and causes all sorts of associated ill health for you, and the people who love you.

Isn't it time to put aside selfish action and consider those others who love us, want the best for us, and are being hurt by standing by, unable to help, watching as healthy life is being squandered away.

So if you reach for a cigarette—see if you can "think" before acting.

Visualise it now:

As your hand reaches for a cigarette, see your hand as bright green, with orange spots, and as you take out a cigarette, see it writhing with maggots and worms, and purple hissing smoke. Realise that if you put the cigarette to your lips, *you*_are being responsible for feeding yourself maggots, worms and purple hissing smoke, which will eat your insides away.

11) WHEN THE URGE BECOMES REALLY STRONG:

When the urge to smoke is a physical reaction which *seems* almost unbearable, take the most immediate time you can to stop what you are doing. Know that this is the most crucial time; the most testing time. And your brain will now be doing all out battle with your mind. Your brain in desperation may have engaged your body on its side for heavyweight outright battle.

Your body and your brain can be controlled by your mind. It may not seem like it now. The brain gives out its message: I must have a cigarette. Give me a cigarette now. When you have given in to my demands, I will be quiet and not pester you further.

Then the brain brings in the heavy mob, the body. It directs the body: Act sick; have a headache, be miserable, have a craving, feel ill, don't concentrate, shake, sweat, fear breathing. Know that just one little puff will take all this away—Body just use your hands, just take a cigarette . . . .

This is the major impact scene for the Mind to enter— NOW: **NO!**

Now brain—who do you think is running this show? Alright you have the capacity to manufacture chemicals and hormones to monitor, even manipulate the body, but if "I" the mind make an alternative suggestion strongly enough—I can override the outcome of your instruction, so ultimately I HAVE THE POWER.

Body, know you will get through this.

YOU HAVE MY HELP.

YOU ARE IN CONTROL.

YOU CAN BE HEALTHY.

YOU ARE WINNING.

WE ARE WINNING—

I AM WINNING—

I AM SUCCEEDING—

I HAVE DEFEATED YOU.

I HAVE ACHIEVED MY GOAL!

I AM A HEALTHY NON-SMOKER.

CONGRATULATIONS!

FIVE MINUTES TO SPARE— HOW TO MAKE IT PRODUCTIVE

Whilst waiting for a computer to load, a kettle to boil, food to cook, waiting for children to come out of school, a traffic jam to clear, waiting to meet a friend, waiting for a return call, literally Five minutes, even four can be made productive or restful—but not irritatingly wasted by unproductive thoughts or flicking through screens on a website, or myriad TV channels. If you really want to achieve some of the things you never get time for, make a brief start with the Five minutes between things which occur during your day.

Have an open crossword nearby and complete a clue

Water your plants

Tidy your desk/drawer/sharpen your pencils

Say a prayer

Really concentrate on a happy uplifting thought

Go outside or look from a window and really see the sky, clouds, sun, flowers, weeds, walls, roads—look at the colours and shades, the sparkle of the rain.

Drawing—recapture a childhood moment—make a list of what you need, get it, do it. Don't be put off the task by making a difficult choice of paper or types of paint. Make an immediate start using the other side of printed paper, or a cheap notebook, and children's paints and a brush, a box of coloured pencils. Wherever you are find a shape and draw it. Change its position and draw it again. Just put pencil to paper. Just do it. It is a start. It's your start and you are trying to do what you want to do. That's it. Five minutes. Keep the book, paper and pencils at hand, for when the next five minutes occur.

Do something with every few minutes, even if it's thinking about what you can draw or paint.

Put a dictionary near you and find five words you've not come across before—look how they are spelt—write them down—remember their meaning and construct a sentence using the word (this helps you to remember them).

Exercise
Point your toes
Stretch your arms down the side of your body
Scrunch your face
Stick out your tongue
Clench and unclench your hands
Go up and down on to your toes
Turn around
Walk backwards

Bend your knees
Sing a song
Hum a tune

Breathe
In through the nose
Out through the mouth
Deep into the stomach
Change the pattern—out through the nose, in through the mouth

Make a list
Of what you need to buy
What you need to do
What you want to do

Update your diary
List what you need to do during the next week
Pencil in 15 minutes for you

Never let a bit of idle time get away. Don't let the easy options like flicking through a magazine, emailing a bit of trivia, scanning TV channels for something that takes your eye. When you have to do these things, allot a chunk of time to yourself to do this, say Five minutes only—schedule in your passive indulgent time, but don't let it spill over into every Five minutes you find.

Use Five minutes to be silent, or still, or to think of nothing in particular consciously knowing that this is important time for you to spend. The trick here is to have focused, silent thought, (meditation), so that your mind is refreshed.

But don't let the time slip by with no productive outcome from it.

Your awareness is the key here. By *choosing* to spend five minutes between the constraints of everything else you have to do, you can consciously apply yourself to making a start on the many things you *want* to achieve.

Of course, you can consciously rest at ease, doing nothing in particular if you wish to, just letting time slip by, at another time which you have designated solely for that purpose.

Time has a habit of slipping by, filled with trivia, whilst accomplishing little. When you feel you've achieved even just a start on something you have wanted to tackle for a long time, your day will feel more satisfying and you will be able to smile inside at your achievement.

It wouldn't be at all surprising if the Five minutes become ten, and longer still, as the sense of accomplishment spreads its positive influence throughout your mind and body.

Great things are achieved from small beginnings. A precious Five minutes spent focused on something of your choice, will gradually help you achieve the goals which have been niggling you, wanting to be heard, and given expression.

Just take Five—you owe it to yourself.

Best of luck!

SECTION 2

IS IT POSSIBLE

THE RIDDLE

Do you know me?

You will eventually. Some day. It is inevitable.

If we've never met, then you do not exist.

For I have always been there—before you were born, and forever after.

I know you.

I have infinite patience. In fact I have infinite time.

I wait. I am a service. Always there, always ready. I could never let you down because you need me, and my only need of you is to serve.

You will look around to find me. Alas I cannot be seen.

I am your haven and respite from the world, and you can enter me, as I have always been able to enter you.

I reside in the most obscure places, and yet also in the most immediate. You could travel miles to find me, and yet I am with you all the time.

When we meet it will be like a homecoming.

But it will not be easy at first. You will doubt me because you cannot see me. I do not have physical form. And this will make you suspicious, even anxious. I do not mind at all. However you locate and receive me will be enough. When you have revealed your readiness, I will be there waiting for you.

You will have expectations, timescales and urgent matters demanding your time. But my response may not be what you expect. Your questions will not be met with responses you will easily understand.

And you may give up. Certainly you will be frustrated. Well I get frustrated too.

Oh sorry, you were perhaps beginning to think that I was some passive, unemotional, balanced, benign spiritual being whose infinite patience and invisibility contains itself in a perfect existence free of strife.

Oh no my friend think again. I exist as part of nature itself. As I become your catalyst, believe me, you do become mine too.

You have so much that I don't have. And yet we share so much. You have a voice that can be heard physically on your plane of existence. It can be used in beautiful melody, or harmful aggression and all the notes in between.

Actually, you've made me think. I too have that capacity, but you will have to learn another language. And yes, you will bother; it is inevitable. You will find me. You will want to. And I am dearly wanting to meet you too.

So where shall we meet?

Well, you could travel. Yes, that would be good because then I could travel too and, through you, see all the wonderful things I already know about. And there may be fleeting moments in the midst of your travels when we will be the closest of companions, awed by some incredible sight or experience, and we will know each other well.

You could locate yourself in the middle of a busy city. I can be there with you. The peace of my vibration is protected from the noise and clamour of urban living, but yours is less so at this time. My voice will be strong, but you will hear it faintly.

Quietness, peace, open air, serenity may be best. The coast, the sea, nature. Yes, this may be your best bet. But don't expect too much.

Planes fly over-head; dogs and children like the outdoors too; lawnmowers and diggers are part of your world. Your peace may be shattered. But I will still be there with you.

Seek a cave, a monastery, church or island. Go where you feel most at ease and relaxed and wait. I will be there.

However, to communicate we need clarity. And there is so much disturbance in your world, causing interruption and lack of concentration.

Do you know that your other constant companion, your ego, does just as good a job, as noise. Just as you get down to quietly thinking, your ego takes this as a good time to send you messages of importance to do with your 'real' life. Food to cook, doors to shut, ironing to do and is that the tap dripping?

So, just as I get you all to myself, your world interferes and our work is put off for another millennium. It makes me quite miffed!

What do you think I do all day? Sit around and wait? Well actually, yes, I do. That is the existence I have been assigned to, and maybe it's just as well, or there would be more disturbance in your world.

Why is there never any peace in your world?

Why is it so difficult to hear my voice?

You alone give me existence.

I exist because I am part of nature, infinite and timeless and I am always there.

You can devise all means for the preparation of the place and time of our meeting and I will always show up, but our rendezvous may not be successful at first, but we will succeed eventually. Expectations are worldly, and time measured outcomes are of your world, not mine.

So if we exist on different planes, what possible benefit can I be to you? Why should you invest your valuable time on earth trying to communicate with a physically non-existent entity that is difficult to communicate with? Why should you even trouble yourself to meet me?.

For goodness sake, you've only got my word so far that I exist!

But I will tell you why, my friend.

I can really help you.

Even if you are successful in human terms, please believe me, every single one of us needs what I can offer.

So now it is time to reveal a little of me.

I am a facilitator. A helper. A means of connecting with a deeper part of you.

Through my vibration, unbounded knowledge and wisdom is poured and directed with an astounding accuracy in a form which you could understand.

Imagine. All knowledge is out there, and through my vibrational frequency you could have access. Your equipment is the receptor, but most times your receiver is faulty.

Your equipment, by the way, is your ears, eyes, brain, mind and ego, all of which get in the way of your reception.

But you could improve this situation, and if you try, all of the powerful forces around you will work unstintingly and magically to transform your receiver to a finely tuned instrument picking up these messages. Your input has to be perseverance. But mainly—are you ready for this—openness and awareness.

I am not an incessant talker. In fact the messages which are transmitted through me are often a few words or a symbol. All you have to do is *listen*. And keep practicing listening.

That's all there is to it.

Simple.

I could leave it there. My work is done.

I've described what I am, where you could find me, how you can find me, and why you will want to, and what benefit you will have when we meet.

I could leave it there. You have all the keys, all the messages. The rest is up to you!

Just listen . . . .

But do you know something? I've got to like you . . . and you could help me too.

During the whole course of your life you will be seeking answers.

Look no further than me.

I am the facilitator who has been designated the honour of serving your purpose on earth, by being the medium to channel vast banks of information and experience, tailored to your needs, via a few words, or symbols, which will have meaning for you alone: Truth.

No subjectiveness. Truth, immaculately translated into your vocabulary. Imagine that.

What's far better is to experience it.

Be open and receptive to the messages that come through to you, via me.

Believe me, your ego would like a piece of the action. Lock it out! He is not welcome. In a clever guise he will be masked as your keeper. Well he is—he locks you up! In order to protect, in order to control, in order to use your mind for limited purpose. So lock him out!

You are being offered a link for your progress and betterment here and in the hereafter. I am the facilitator to provide the connection for the answers you seek.

Talking of me briefly (perhaps I have an alter-ego!) I will finally reveal my identity—although you've probably guessed already and in your heart already know.

I am **SILENCE**.

I am always with you. I have infinite time and can serve you anywhere. I am portable so you don't have to travel to find me. But wherever we meet, as your true companion when you receive my messages, your life will take on clear meaning.

No more now . . . . Shhh! Shhh! . . . Shhh! Silence . . . .

DEW

Picture this.

It's getting lighter. Somewhere, low on the horizon the sun is rising in the sky. The coolness of night is slipping into the warming of day. Whilst you slept, tremendous happenings occurred for your delight and pleasure, and for the continuation and evolution of life on earth.

Your heard no sound.

In an unfathomable science, nature birthed me. I was conceived as the coolness of the night kissed the warmth of morning. I was drawn out, given purpose and shape and placed on a blade of grass for creations' purpose.

Millions of us were born at the same time, as it has always been, due to the balance of nature. Vitalised by sun and water I have potentialised to the whole of what I was decreed to become. I now sit poised delicately at the end of a blade of grass, unconcerned at my fate, except that I change form and am linked to the essence of my nature in diverse ways during the cycles of my existence.

Not unlike you perhaps?

Yet we are so different.

I have a simple intelligence, but no brain, no power of reasoning, no voice. My existence is to potentialise, to be that which I am. Only that.

Your freedom of choice prevents you doing that.

I have no choice. Nature commands, dictates, and I comply because there is no other way.

This morning I have had a unique experience.

Singled out to be encountered at close range, I did my very best to shine and sparkle. The global unit that I am had a moment of glory borne of sun and water and the diamond brilliance of my moisture-filled body glistened with rainbow colours merely for your pleasure.

Oh and furthermore, when your eyes rested on the carpet at your feet, as one nation, captured in that moment of sunlight, we all turned our bodies into prisms of dancing, sparkling, diamond light for a hidden reason.

Perhaps to make you think. Think what? Philosophically, perhaps. About major and minor. Infinity. Unity and uniqueness. The marvels of nature. To stir your imagination. To awaken your spirit. To turn a mundane moment into an enlivening experience.

Anyway, there I am, poised on this blade of grass. Me and thousands like me, awaiting our fate as the sun warms us, shrinks and evaporates us, lifting us in changed form, heavenward, to meet our cousins of vapour from vastly different areas. To combine us as a new unit of moisture, held in the bodies of fluffy, turbulent cloud, before another fate calls us . . .

Anyway, there I am poised, when suddenly thousands of us are crushed in one fell swoop, and as the pounding recedes, we have burst into each other becoming the dampened mess of a human footprint! We do not shriek with fear. Fluidity is our nature, and absorption is our fate. So human form meets nature's mystery and a pathway through the dew-laden lawn is testament to the mingling and sparkling energy exchange which has taken place.

We are always at the mercy or service of other life. This is our purpose—to provide moisture and great delight to the insects, birds and humans alike and this great mystery of a life short lived and often missed or taken for granted is our part in the great Gaia of life.

Today, by recognition, gratitude was expressed, and we can rest happily in our existence knowing that there was a moment of unity in the world.

With love from a drop of dew!

I WANT TO KNOW WHY

I want to know why the grass is green,

Why the words I speak cannot be seen.
Why ears can hear, and eyes can see,
And yet I cannot look at me.
I want to know why the moon, up there,
Can hang so still in the evening air.
And if from the sky it were to fall,
Could I hold it like a ball?

I want to know why a cat has fur,
Why it doesn't speak and can only purr.
Why a dog can bark and wag it tail,
And a shell belongs on the back of a snail.

I want to know why a spider swings
On a thread of web—it has no wings.
I want to know where a ladybird goes,
When I tread on its back with my five little toes.

I want to know why Mummy's smile turns to frown,
When my bowl of porridge lands upside-down.
And why she shouts and then gets mad,
And then hugs me to her, when she is sad.

I want to know why I must use a spoon.
When my fingers taste good—I will learn soon.
I want to know why I can't throw cake,
Or jump on my Daddy to make him wake.

I want to know why when I touch a bubble,
It bursts and is gone—Life is such a trouble!
I want to know why I must pick up my toys,
And why when I want to, I can't make a noise!

I want to know why I must play with my friend.
He's got all my toys—I don't want to lend!

That cake mummy's making looks too good to eat;
Could I just give it a kick with my feet? . . .
Though I'm strapped in this chair, I want to know why,
Now that cake's on the floor, I am going to cry!

FLYING ANTS

Alright, alright! I know you think I'm not attractive.

I know I tickle and annoy.

But give me a chance. You're not the only one who lives on this planet you know.

You have years. I only have hours. Life is precarious for us.

We have to leave our natural habitat and go elsewhere with a precious mission.

It may be safe sex on your plane, but nothing is safe in our world.

Our existence relies on nature's combination more than yours. If it's not right we don't exist.

Of course, when it is right—we triumph in swarms, some of us getting into hidden crevices to multiply.

I even heard of one successful mission where thousands of us were hatched on the inside of a window pane. Well done, that was. No interference for many hours. Boy, did we show them how we colonize!

What became of them, you ask?

Oh for goodness sake, can't you let us have our time of glory. Well I don't know . . . well I've forgotten . . . Oh blast! We were wiped out, literally, by that upstart nation of humans who have the upper hand on this planet!

That's always our problem. We are sent off with a mission. We evolve, we have wings, we fly (and it's pretty scary I can tell you). A land-based insect given wings, hurtling about in the air! No leaves, no grass nor soil to cling to. Oh no you just get your orders and off you go. It's a wonder we arrive anywhere at all. Humans are always vigilant to swot us and diminish our ranks. Birds think we are fast food. The wind plays havoc with our direction, and then suddenly, splat! What you thought you could fly through, turns out to be glass, and good-bye brother—he never made it!

Okay. Okay. So you don't like us. The feeling is mutual you know. Take a look at yourselves—long spindly legs, all different shapes and colours, no beautiful wings. You try flying. Go on. Clumsy aren't you?

What's our purpose in life? I might well ask you the same thing.

I could hazard a guess at ours.

To spread annoyance, disruption and distaste to your comfortable homes and lives.

And why not? You have it too easy.

We are the ones whose lives are on the line. With fly sprays and insect repellents. Who gives us a break?

For a few brief hours we come into existence—and maybe you can't fathom out why, but then neither can we.

We were dealt the losing hand you know. Would you want to be a flying ant? No. Well neither do I.

But what choice do I have. Get up and fly—that's what I'm programmed to do.

If only I could have been a regular soldier ant!

But no, here I am. With my smart brothers in our black livery and silver wings, sharing a little bit of nature's earth, unwelcome as we are—except to the birds, who love us as scrumptious morsels! Just part of the food chain!

So don't give us a hard time.

We'll be gone sooner than you think.

However, when we are around, we can cause a bit of havoc and inconvenience! Great!

THE STONE BUDDHA

Poised.
Silent.
Still.
In all weathers.

Something of the spirit I personify emanates from my inanimate stance.

You know this because near me you will feel calm and unhurried. Almost like entering a dimension out of sync with the rest of the world.

I have no nature, no personality belonging to me, no needs, no desires, no emotions.

I am as unlike you as it is possible to get. And yet you could wish to have the stillness, peace and silent communication I have.

I have been created by man, both in physical aspect and imaginative projection.

The form I express is flow. Flowing garments, roundness, balance, wisdom. How so from a lump of stone? It is the representation of form which reaches you. You give me life and purpose.

Because I am in the form of a Deity, my power calls to you.

Even plants bask in my presence; nature is at peace because of an etheric imprint emanating from my form!

Seeing everything with unseeing eyes, my form has been revered in legend for thousands of years. I sit still and at peace because my form is imprisoned in stone. The mysticism I represent calls you to prayer and meditation.

When I am in your life as a representation of flow and peace, I will add that quality to your thinking.

Buddha—your imagination and memory gives me life.

Yet I am formed in stone, nothing else.

Isn't that amazing?

THE OVERLY PRACTICAL GUIDE TO PARENTING

My 'tongue in cheek' guide aims to illustrate why wise parents stop at two children and why even wiser ones, having read my true-life guide, consider seriously whether to jump on the proverbial band-wagon and go ahead anyway!

If whilst reading this no-nonsense, realistic paper, you are actually pregnant—don't worry too much—unless this is your third child (in which case feel free to scream), but in any case sequels entitled "How to Manage One—Never Feel Guilty About the Only Child" and "Two's Too Many", may well be demanded shortly!

This guide will deal with simple everyday occurrences like the family meal, toilet training and bedtime, and in that order as from my experience you will be eventually eating with your child (after steps 1-40 have been progressed through)—when he will want to go to the toilet (steps 1-7) and this will result in your sending him to bed! (steps 1 to infinity). However don't be alarmed if your child is not up to standard, by putting you to test on all the diagnosed steps—he may just be a perfect angel and you the perfect parents. The rest of us just slog away day to day trying to be!

One last thing—this is the perfect article to slip in front of newly-weds and couples planning (or not planning!) to have children, as it will certainly make them think hard before sewing the seed of their imagined "perfect family". No home should be without a copy for ease of reference at one of those tricky situations—and I predict it will replace all literature along the lines of "How to deal with Temper Tantrums" by Patience Honey and "Bringing up Children the Easy Way" by Joy Loveless! (Should these two people actually exist, I'd love to meet them!)

A final word—If increasing the size of your family is on your mind, and you have not yet read this guide (and therefore have not deferred your decision to go ahead), let me give you a word of advice. Read as many helpful books as you can on the psychology of bringing up a child— let the facts sink in and then forget them, or you will be overburdened with your sense of guilt for not reaching the exacting standards expected of the normal, rational, patient, knowledge-seeking, game-playing parents of this era such as we! It is during a crisis when you wallow in guilt for not having handled the situation better, that you will automatically reach out for the comfort of this guide and be mightily relieved to find solace in the knowledge that none of us is perfect! And others (me for one), have been through the same experiences and sympathise fully!

Such is its potency for birth-control that you will more than likely pick up a copy of this guide in a Chemists next to the Durex Gossamers, rather than a book shop!

As expressed, this article covers coping (just!) with three children.

We will assume that One was easy; Two (well who noticed the extra one), but Three—that magic number that jolts everyone to the realisation—stark and bold—I have THREE children! It is as though the accumulation of extra noise, toys, clothes and work crept up quietly and unnoticeably until number Three became a little person in his own right. Then suddenly the world was brought into focus with surprise that's hard to believe.

Whether planned or not, number Three is special. Lying there in early infancy all quiet and peaceful and the best baby yet—but hold on, he is about to take the world by storm. Oh yes, he fits into routines well, is the easiest to manage and life is idyllic—two elder siblings to play with and amuse him, to clear up his toys and stay with him outside the shops, but wait—one day he wakes up and he is two!

Then reality hits hard—he demands to be heard, has a mind of his own and doesn't want to play with his elders! Suddenly you have THREE children. And it didn't just take 9 months—it took two years 9 months!

MEALTIMES!

Firstly a list of requirements to cover all eventualities at mealtimes.

Change of clothes—you and he

One bib—big, washable, with sleeves and pocket for catching food, which ties at the back

One huge ground sheet (approximately the size of the whole room and walls!)—I joke not. However as this may be impractical I advise alternatives:

1) Put child and high chair in the garden (unless winter)

2) Try to sit him at least 5 meters away from anything you want to protect including other members of the family; hair; etc

3) Stand guard with brush, face cloth and extra spoons and just hover until the meal is complete.

A bottle of Tomato Ketchup—no family should be without one (unless allergy is apparent and indeed shares in a proprietary brand would be well worth investing in), as this accompaniment to every meal enables you to feel that he has successfully eaten something. Aids such as this should be marked POMFP (Peace of Mind For Parents)

Extra fork, spoon, cup of drink, and alternatives to the food offered.

A table large enough so that his little legs, sticking straight out from a big chair do not kick or otherwise molest the other members of the family.

Before you actually sit down, take him to the toilet. He will not want to go then of course, but you will be able to say to yourself—I did try!

Then put on his bib. As he squirms about not wanting to push his arms into the armholes, take your mind from the scene he is causing to glance at the milk about to boil over, or the toast burning to a beautiful deep mahogany shade. Distraction during one crisis helps you to spot another pending!

Make sure his bib, minus long hair, is tied securely at the back, so that trick-playing conspirators, i.e. his brothers and sisters, can't undo it too easily. Then again, not too tightly in case immediate release is needed—like when he is finished and gets down, spilling the contents of the bib, or rubbing it all over your nice clean dress as he brushes past!

Now sit him on his chair. Do NOT keep him waiting for his food. This could result in unbelievable catastrophe. Whilst you spoon out his meal, back turned to him and eyes averted for a few minutes, the whole table could be totally devastated. Signs to listen for: Silence, then a satisfied giggle—he has tipped all the salt over the table. Cups clanking—he has drunk the milk set out for your welcome cup of tea! Or trickling water (and try to take this calmly)—either it's the fifth cup of orange juice today he has knocked over, or yes, your instinct was right, he didn't ask to go to the toilet.

In all cases steps are necessary to have the meal in front of him as he sits down.

Now come his demands. Salt? Well, against your better judgement, yes he can have a microscopic amount. After all everyone else does—how do you explain to a two year old that he cannot have any, when he sees with his own eyes that it must be good as everyone else has some. So a little salt—he's the independent type who wants to do it himself? OK, as you hover on tenter hooks, hoping he will give it back when you say so, he delights in making long white trails over his plate—when you actually pull it out of his grasp, having run out of time and patience saying "Now give it to mummy", the top comes off, scattering salt everywhere, much to the amusement/annoyance of his brothers and sisters.

Having mopped up the excess salt, you can proceed to pepper, tomato sauce etc. Much along the same lines—but beware MUSTARD. Mustard is HOT—particularly English Mustard. But it is bright yellow and attractive and there's no steam coming from it to confirm it's temperature and No. Three wants some like everyone else. So a little bit, is tentatively put on the side of the plate. Forget dipping the chips into it, he uses the spoon (for the first time ever, despite your persuasion to do so in other circumstances), and suddenly he bursts into tears. "It's burning", and no amount of water will eradicate the memory that the meal—not the mustard, burnt his tongue. So the rest of the meal is a no-go zone.

But now he is ready for his pudding (just as you cut into your long-awaited juicy steak, which has now gone cold), and he demands pudding and wee-wee all in the same breath. In exasperation you will count to ten, smile sweetly and grab his wrists marching him off to the loo.

If you are ultra-efficient you will of course have stopped to wipe the debris of the meal from his bib, otherwise a trail to the toilet will inevitably follow you. Now undo the bib. (Here is where the perfect knot comes in!), take off his jumper, undo his braces, pull down his pants, and hold his little handle down!

A word is necessary here for adults ignorant of the importance of "angle of dangle" because resulting wet pants and floor, happily sprayed by a warm fountain, results in Extra Work. Not just mopping up. But in finding a clean, dry pair of pants as a spot of moisture in "Big Boys Pants" is enough to arouse the "Refusal to Co-Operate" Syndrome, characterised by rolling around on the floor, kicking legs and screaming.

So, assuming by practice you have now mastered the art of sitting him on the toilet, you can wash your hands, and his of course. Yes, and soap. And Yes he can dry them himself; put on his jumper, trousers and bib and lead him back to the table.

Meanwhile, despite all the rumpus you heard from the kitchen whilst you were otherwise engaged, the other two have finished. Well, that's there term for it, though it is far short of your interpretation of the word. And they are ready for their pudding.

When three of them start talking at once—the loudest usually winning—and between your own hurried mouthfuls, you try to control the antics of one who can't sit still and keeps falling off his chair, and another who refuses to leave his spoon quietly on the table, preferring to bounce its end against the knife, and the third flicking bits of spaghetti into an imaginary goal, you do at this point wonder why you ever bothered!

Once the meal is over, and your lovely brood is picking up their toys (some hope!), you can scour the kitchen, clean the food from crevices in the chairs, wipe finger prints off the seats and walls, and wash up. This will become a delightful interlude believe me—minutes of peace and bubbles where your mind drifts away, suddenly brought back to reality with a wailing . . . . "They made funny faces at me!" There really is no answer to this, except thankfully it is bed time.

Give at least 10 minutes warning, and get that bath exactly the right temperature. If you are in a hurry, or just want them to have some time together, three is still a number that works in the bath. But being the youngest, and soonest to bed, Number Three must come out first, and he really doesn't want to, even though the other two spread out taking up all the room, and squeal when he treads on them. Despite noisy protest, he is tired and wrapped in a towel looking all pink and gorgeous, he becomes your little angel again.

However being two, nearly three, the angel and the demon are quite easily interchangeable. And by the time his pyjamas are on, and each and every toy which has a particular place in his bed, is recovered from hiding places all around the house, he is ready for a story.

Be careful in your choice of book—not too scary, not one he has read before, and one that doesn't take too much time to read, as you will be required somewhere else, to perform similar duties. His drinking cup better be by the bed, his teeth should have been cleaned and favourite teddy, or monkey or other fluffy animal, or truck, better be in the right order, as any one of these omissions will result in delaying tactics, when you finally think that the coast is clear for you to leave.

Long eyelashes resting on a soft pink face, clean and peaceful and finally quiet, you are rewarded for your devotion to duty with a sigh of satisfaction that this dear sleeping boy is your pride and joy! Not to mention that you got through the day in one piece!. Just!

Now, for your husband . . . .

ANOTHER RIDDLE

I am unique. There is only one
And yet I am owned by everyone.
A miracle of rare design
I twist and twirl, yet follow a line.
You can see me and yet,
When I'm at my best
As a signature mark,
I prove the test.
For What I am,
Tells me I'm You.
There's no mistake,
My identity's true.
Recognise me by looking hard,
But you'll never remember . . .
Put me on a card.
Dip me in ink,
My form to reveal,
And then your fate,
My presence will seal.

(A finger print)

JUST ONE MORE . . .
Stuck still in an anchor
Yet travelling far,
I spin and I hurtle
Yet never get far.
Away from companions,
Yet joined at my base,
You cannot know the strain
As I race,
Over bumps and stones on the path in my way
And yet if I falter there's a price to pay.
If I cracked and broke
On my daily run,
Disaster would strike
It would be no fun.
For though I am small
Only one of a few
Without me there'd be
No travel at all.

(The spoke of a wheel)

SECTION 3
THINKING DEEPLY

Gradually Forgetting

Time

Life

GRADUALLY FORGETTING

Memory hides behind a curtain—but which one?

Come out memory, I've had enough of hide and seek.

I need you NOW: Why desert me when my sanity relies on you?

Memory, you've chosen a crucial time to be on holiday. Pass the work to Recall, and you can return to your vacation!

How could I forget things that I've Known!

A breeze blows through confusion, scattering thought. Logic departs. Debris disappears.

Eyes observe. Mind conveys. Lips muddle words.

Nets in the mind, catch stray thoughts. Incoherent speech.

Mind clutter. Confusion speaks. Words unexpressed.

Silent mind. Screaming outrage. Anger expressed.

Memory anchors thought. So that going far, it may return.

Fact is not irrelevant. It is irreverent.

Inhale interruption. Exhale exasperation.

Details unobserved run down the page like watercolour thought. Oils fix thoughts indelibly.

Doubts are cast on a restless sea. Turmoil.

Shards of memory fly from the oceans depth, and land hard on the ship of life. Smack! Knocked senseless, out of their depth.

Will I recall my future, when it becomes my past.

Who am I? My memories have forgotten me, but I am still me, breathing and alive.

Spontaneous thoughts trip on the mouth, spouting confusion.

Random thought expressed, like sparkling water, can blind the beholder.

Inaudible words mask the man; naked, female intuition interprets.

Be Heard, screams the mind. Recollection escapes. But only in bits.

A thrush sings, or was it a woodpecker—even birds get it wrong!

Memory fading, link by link. Was the chain of thought which secured my knowledge, so rusty?

Have I been important enough to be remembered?

I was present as my memories were being made. But where is my memory now? Lost in the past!

Striving to be heard, words amass. Energy pours out. Only thought is frugal.

Silently, frustration is felt. Angrily, frustration is expressed. When was this condition born?

One day my memory will return; until then, I am in pieces.

When urgent re-call is needed, I find the office on vacation.

The memory plays tricks, and I was never a magician, but was I once a musician?

Departing memories slip away like dreams being recalled. Once substantial, they are now flimsy, like gossamer. The fabric of life, once so taught, is now fraying.

Net of memories, which caught my history, now has a hole too big—the details are escaping.

Where was my mind when I needed it to record facts. It was out enjoying life, blissfully unaware that these would prove to be important.

I never grew up. It was more important then to enjoy the feel of the sun, the sensation of discovery, the pleasure of experience to log the where, or the when.

Busy enjoying the why and how, I missed the when and where.

I once knew and could say, who and where an image was.

My memories are vacating—where are we going?

Because I cannot recall, only makes me look stupid. I am still me. Inside. Where I don't know what is happening.

Once I gave memory no thought; now it returns the recklessness.

In mind a single vision. In speech a hundred words. But peripheral speech does not exact the image.

Concise speech requires a clear mind. But mine is foggy with all but the right words.

Families unite. Friction speaks. Bonds unravel. Freedom speaks.

Welcome night falls, covering our faults. But morning comes.

Stones in the mind, weigh life down. Feathers tickle the senses. Laughter.

Love casts nets on the sea of life, bringing forth delicious fishes!

Love endures. Hope reigns. Frustration felt.

TIME

Time is transient.

With no trauma it carries us towards trauma.

Time remains; is always; never changes; is undeniably always there.

We move through time.

Time is not a moment, nor a day.

It is a certainty, even when we are not here, Time remains.

Time glides into infinity from infinity.

We weave our way across its measure, eventually ourselves to become timeless.

Time is an invisible essence: boundless, yet binding.

Our time is our life, measured by human comprehension.

LIFE

What is life?

Life is the time we exist in physical form.

In our life, we are tested, our accomplishments are measured. Our achievements and strengths exposed. Our human form to age, and our knowledge to grow.

What use is knowledge in our life, if it should disappear when our physical form is gone?

Are writers of knowledge the saviours in our life, who pass on wisdom to unknowledgeable minds?

Knowledge is only ever in part. The wisest man knows only to the extent of the experience of his time; his life.

What of those of us, whose lives change no course, cause no new discovery, whose fates appear to serve no crusade?

What of us millions who cross time's tapestry, affecting only modestly the lives of those whose paths we cross?

Surely each of us makes a contribution to the Whole.

Surely the knowledge of each human mind is gathered, through the spirit—that invisible and often unbelievable presence which exists even when our limited comprehension believes we no longer do exist.

Perhaps the knowledge is sorted and reallocated to new born souls, or is added to a growing, infinitesimal wholeness, whose purpose is incomprehensible to us.

For why is our vision limited to the dimension of a measured vista? Why is our hearing deafened beyond a measured decibel?

Our senses allow us to exist in this world of limited dimensions. If we comprehended powers beyond those which allow us to exist in this life, would the quest for their attainment be beyond the purpose of our worldly existence?

Disbelievers use logic to be their captors, insisting that only the proven is real. They are safe within their dimensional awareness.

A few catch a glimpse beyond regular human comprehension.

But what of the potential knowledge hidden within parts of the brain to which we have no access at the present undeciphered as yet by mankind's ingenious, mechanical computers? The signals, codes, flashes of light, as yet meaningless, soon to be discovered perhaps, or always to remain a mystery, as illusive as man's search is penetrating.

Perhaps these atoms of sequenced light contain the essence of our existence, their range at present beyond our powers of enlightenment.

Perhaps these messages link us to the wholeness to which our lives contribute their knowledge.

And perhaps through this link we are linked to each other, our fates already determined for some specific cause which we need not know, but are inescapably propelled towards for the perpetuation of life on this planet.

Herein lies our time—and within that time—**OUR LIFE**.

BIOGRAPHY FOR PEBBLES

Julie Ann Smith

With her family and secretarial background and numerous interests ranging from metaphysics to practical philosophy, yoga to crystals and gardening to psychology, and a passion for travel, *Pebbles* has been the culmination of a selection of articles, written throughout the author's life, to explore the dilemmas and humour of everyday living.

From hot-air ballooning in Australia, to white water rafting on the Kawarau in New Zealand, to abseiling in the Lake District and snaking through the Chu Chi tunnels in Vietnam, she loves life—doing it, seeing it, exploring it and experiencing it!

Living near the rugged coast of Cornwall with her husband, she is currently experimenting with playing the key board, watercolour painting and freelance writing, whilst awaiting more adventures in the Caribbean and, later in the year, in Peru.

The fortunately rich diversity of her life has created the unique insights which are *Pebbles*.